BY THE EDITORS OF
CONSUMER GUIDE®

PRACTICAL GUIDE TO
DOG CARE

Sheldon Rubin, DVM

Publications International, Ltd.

About the Author: Sheldon Rubin, DVM, is a practicing veterinarian in Chicago, Illinois. He received his Doctorate of Veterinary Medicine from the University of Illinois and served as President of the Chicago Veterinary Medical Association. He is a member of the American Animal Hospital Association, the American Veterinary Medical Association, and the Anti-Cruelty Society.

Cover Photo: Seide Preis Photography

CONTENTS

Introduction

Dogs and humans have been friends for centuries—from the time when humans learned to value the dog's skills as hunter and guardian, to the present day when the companionship of a dog is recognized as a source of deep pleasure and satisfaction to millions of people.

Some dogs still perform the tasks of their ancestors: guarding property, herding cattle, hunting game. Some work for their living as police or guide dogs. But today your wish to own a dog is more likely to spring from an appreciation of the generous companionship a dog can give. So deep, in fact, is the friendship that can exist between a person and a pet that scientists have given it a name. They call it the human/companion animal bond, and they say that owning a pet helps you feel good, get along with other people, and even live longer.

What makes the dog such a good friend? It's loyal, social, demonstrative. And it doesn't even ask a lot in return—except, of course, your love and loyalty in exchange for its. What else does your dog ask of you? Food and shelter, certainly. Regular grooming and exercise. Routine health care. Medical care if it's necessary.

This book tells how to be your dog's best friend. It discusses everything from choosing the dog that will be happy in your household, to feeding, grooming, and training your dog, to getting along with the veterinarian and knowing what to do in an emergency.

CHOOSING YOUR DOG: FINDING A FRIEND

The original relationship between dogs and human beings was a working relationship. Dogs herded sheep and cattle, pulled sleds or carts, protected people and their food supply against predators, and retrieved the game shot by hunters. Working dogs still sometimes perform these tasks, but these days it's more likely that you'll want a dog for companionship than for a specific working assignment.

People And Dogs: A Social Relationship

Anyone who has owned a dog knows that a dog is a good and loyal friend. And the dog is a social animal. It adjusts easily to your lifestyle; nothing pleases it more than to please you. It'll take part enthusiastically in your life and that of your family and ask for nothing in return except your care and affection. In times of stress, the uncritical friendship of a dog can help defuse the tension and calm you down. In fact, after generations of taking the complex human/animal relationship for granted, scientists are now studying the beneficial effects of pet ownership.

As a result of scientific research, there is now

medical evidence to prove that the friendly company of a dog can do some people more good than
sophisticated medications. Scientists have discovered that Americans who own a pet live longer
than those who don't, and that in the act of petting
a dog a person's blood pressure drops. Elderly
people in nursing homes who seem to have lost the
will to live can be brought out of their shells by
having a cat or dog to touch and relate to. Children
with learning disabilities or behavioral problems
often improve dramatically when a pet comes into
their lives.

How do animals help their owners to live longer,
feel better, and get along with their neighbors?
According to scientists:

• A pet is good company and decreases the owner's
sense of loneliness or isolation.

• Taking care of a pet keeps the owner busy.

• Being responsible for an animal's well-being
increases the owner's motivation and interest in
things outside him or herself.

• A pet can be touched, petted, and handled, thus
satisfying a person's emotional need to be in physical contact with another living creature.

Fortunately for you, your dog will instinctively
follow the example of its ancestors as your protec-
tor (after companionship, protection is the most
common reason that people acquire a dog). A dog
has a strong urge to protect its own territory—and
for your dog, that means you and your home. Even

a small dog will bark to warn you of an intruder at the door or on your property. In fact, convicted burglars have said that a small, noisy dog is better protection against intrusion than a large dog that looks ferocious; no criminal likes to have attention drawn to his or her activities. And a large dog at your side when you're out walking is likely to discourage would-be troublemakers.

Understanding Your Dog's Past

The guarding instinct isn't the only working instinct your dog will demonstrate, and you'll find it interesting to note that although many working and sporting dogs are no longer used for the work they were originally called on to do, they retain their instinct to perform. Your Border collie may anxiously circle a group of other dogs, or even children, until it's got them all together in one place; this behavior is a throwback to the job its ancestors were bred to do—herding sheep. Some small breeds, like Welsh corgis, have a tendency to snap at the heels of dogs (or people)—it's the way their ancestors rounded up cattle.

Even if you acquire a mixed-breed dog, you can often make a good guess at its ancestry by watching the way it behaves. And many of these behavioral patterns can be useful clues when you're making a choice about the kind of dog you'd like to have as a pet.

Even before you decide what kind of dog you want, however, you ought to take a good look at why you want a dog at all. Is it for companionship? As a friend for the children? As a guard dog— formally trained to guard or simply to provide a good loud warning bark or an impressive presence? Do you want a dog that you can exhibit at breed shows or obedience trials? Do you plan to breed your dog?

A Long-Term Commitment

Whichever answer you give, remind yourself that *any* dog will make certain demands on you—long-term demands, at that. Any dog, St. Bernard or Pekingese, purebred or mutt, will cost you time, energy, and money. All dogs need food, shelter, and routine medical care—vaccinations, for instance. They get sick and sometimes need specialized care that can be expensive. You'll need leashes and grooming equipment. If you travel, you have to take the dog along or make special arrangements to have it cared for. Moreover, your dog has to be socially acceptable; it's up to you to train it to do as it's told and not be a nuisance to others. This isn't just a courtesy to your neighbors, either; it's illegal to allow a dog to be a nuisance to other people. By law, you must license your dog and get it vaccinated against rabies.

And owning a dog is a long-term commitment. A healthy, small dog may well live 15 years or more. So that bounding puppy playing with the kids will still be around when the kids are off on their own. And it'll still be your responsibility.

What Kind Of Dog Is Right For You?

So do you *really* want a dog? If you've taken a good look at the long-term responsibilities of dog ownership and decided that you're willing and able to take them on, it's time to make the next decision: What kind of a dog is going to fit into your life most satisfactorily? Answer the following questions to help yourself make a decision:

How will the dog fit—literally—into your home?

In other words, what size dog do you want? Very often, circumstances outside your control will answer this question for you. Large dogs take up a lot of space and usually need a lot of exercise (although some small breeds are very lively). If you're living in a small apartment, you can't accommodate that cute puppy when you know that by this time next year it's going to be the size of the sofa. So forget about the St. Bernards and German shepherds and turn your attention to something that's more practical in size—like a toy breed or a terrier.

Who's going to exercise the dog?

As mentioned earlier, most large breeds need regular exercise and lots of it, and some small breeds are a lot more energetic than you might expect. Beagles, for instance, have great stamina and need plenty of exercise. Otherwise, they'll bounce around indoors and drive you crazy. And where will the dog urinate and defecate? Remember that in some areas you're legally responsible for cleaning up after it. Will you have to exercise the dog yourself, or can you recruit family members to do some of it? Do you have a big yard where the dog can play, or must you walk it on a leash to the nearest park when it needs to run? If your space and/or your energy is at a premium, choose a dog that's a natural stay-at-home, not an outdoorsy type.

How much dog can you feed?

All dogs cost money—no matter their size. Routine vaccinations, checkups, licenses, and, in some cases, boarding kennel fees and special grooming needs are inevitable expenses for any dog owner. But it's clearly true that a miniature schnauzer eats less than a German shepherd, so if your budget is tight, do yourself a favor and don't get a dog that's going to eat as much as a small horse.

What about temperament?

Dogs, like people, have different personalities: some are lively, some are lazy; some are high-strung, some aren't ruffled by anything. Decide what sort of dog will be temperamentally suitable for your household. And don't imagine that if you want a "quiet" dog, you've got to pick a small one. Some large breeds, like Labrador retrievers, are usually extremely easygoing and even-tempered. The chart at the end of this chapter lists the characteristic traits of popular breeds of dogs and can help you judge if a certain type is going to be temperamentally suited to you and your family. Which brings you to the next point:

Does the dog like children?

How well a dog gets along with children depends on several issues: heredity, training, past experience, and so on. If you want a dog that's good with kids, you won't choose one that's traditionally short-tempered or snappy—a Chihuahua, for instance. Nor will you choose one that's too timid to be able to cope with boisterous children. If you're getting your pet from a humane shelter, you'll need to check out its temperament carefully. A dog that's been abused or mishandled in the past is less likely to fit in with children than a healthy puppy who has learned to trust humans from its earliest days.

How much work will it be?

An important consideration is how much care a dog needs beyond the obvious considerations like routine grooming and veterinary checkups. Long-haired dogs clearly require more grooming than short-haired dogs; some, like Afghan hounds and Old English sheepdogs, must be groomed every day. Are you willing to do it? And, even if you're willing, do you have the time? If you're on a tight schedule and know you wouldn't have time to exercise a lively young Doberman pinscher, you wouldn't have time to untangle the shaggy coat of an Old English sheepdog, either. As you see, practical considerations inevitably put some limits on your choices. And there's another aspect of your dog's looks that you have to consider: Will maintaining your dog's coat be an added expense? Some breeds require periodical professional grooming and trimming. Are you prepared to make the regular trips to the canine beauty shop? And are you willing to pick up the bill?

There's also the question of shedding. Some long-haired breeds—one is the Norwegian elkhound—have a dense undercoat which traps dead hair. If the dog is not groomed properly, it'll shed for longer periods than is normal. So you'll wind up grooming the rugs and furniture as well as the dog.

You must also consider whether anyone in your family is allergic to dog dander (the dried flakes of skin that fall off when the animal sheds). If so, you'd be better off with a dog that sheds less and is less likely to trigger allergic reactions. Poodles, schnauzers, and Maltese terriers are among breeds that shed little and are well suited to mildly allergic people.

How much do you travel?

Your lifestyle and the amount of traveling you do also affect your choice of a dog. If you're always on the move, however, you've got to consider what you'll do with your dog while you're away. It's easier to pack a dachshund than a Great Dane. You can more easily ask a friend to come in and care for a small dog than one that's used to daily five-mile hikes. And, if you have to board your dog, the rates for a small dog will be lower than for a giant one.

Three Nitty-Gritty Questions

Now you've got a good idea of the *kind* of dog that will fit—for practical, financial, and temperamental purposes—into your household. There are still three nitty-gritty questions to answer:

Do you want a male or female dog?
Do you want a purebred or a mutt?
Do you want a puppy or an adult?

The sex of the dog you want to buy is largely a matter of choice. Neither sex is healthier than the other. Female dogs are somewhat calmer and less excitable than males, but unless you have your female dog spayed, you'll have to keep her confined or well under control during her two yearly fertile or heat periods, which last about three weeks each. Male dogs tend to be more aggressive than females, they tend to roam more, and they sometimes have socially unacceptable habits like trying to "mount" people or marking their territory by urinating on the furniture. Neutering the male dog usually causes these undesirable characteristics to subside.

If you want a dog that you can exhibit in breed (or conformation) shows or obedience trials, then obviously you're looking for a purebred. The actual process of choosing one will be discussed later. Purebred dogs are more costly than mixed breeds—they can be *very* expensive. The rarer the breed, the more expensive it becomes; so if you want the prestige of owning a dog that's a class act, you'll have to pay for it.

Don't, however, make the mistake of buying a dog just because it's unusual. Find out all you can about the breed first. This is not hard to do, because years and years of selective breeding have given dog fanciers a good idea of what to expect from a certain breed in terms of appearance, character, health considerations, and longevity. But there's a catch: indiscriminate or inbreeding has produced dogs that are not representative of the breed, or that have a marked tendency to hereditary defects. It's essential, therefore, to buy a purebred only from a reputable kennel, and to know what you're looking for before you buy your dog.

Apart from status, however, there's no difference between a dog with a pedigree and a dog that's a mixture of breeds. You may find, in fact, that a mutt has inherited the best of all its ancestors.

Do you want a puppy or an adult dog? This can be an emotional decision. Puppies are cute. *All* puppies are cute. If you have kids, they'll probably beg you to get a cute puppy. Remember, though, that you're not buying the dog just for the children. As mentioned earlier, the dog will probably still be around when the children are long gone. And it's always a mistake to succumb and get a puppy for a child who absolutely promises to take care of it all by him or herself. Trying to make a child take on full responsibility for a pet never works. It's unfair to everyone—the child, the dog, and you. When you're tempted, remember the huge numbers of dogs that are put to sleep each year in humane shelters, or that wander the streets without a home. A lot of them started out as puppies some youngster promised to take care of all by himself. Don't take any chances that the cute puppy your kids talk you into buying will turn into a big dog you can't cope with, and will sooner or later wind up among the pathetic army of dogs nobody wants.

Puppies demand a great deal of time, attention, and patience, but there are advantages to getting a dog as a puppy. A puppy who's had no previous experience of living with people will adjust more easily to the routine of your household than an adult dog. It'll know who's boss right from the start. You'll be able to train it yourself, and you won't have to correct any ingrained bad habits. And a puppy that you've loved and cared for from the beginning is likely to grow into a contented, good-tempered dog.

If you'd rather avoid the bouncy puppy stage and get an older dog, it's a good idea to go to a reputable animal shelter or humane society. There's no shortage of dogs available for adoption, and you'll be giving a home to a dog that might otherwise be destroyed. Although you'll know nothing of the dog's parentage, the shelter should be able to alert you to any behavior problems the dog may have as a result of past mismanagement or abuse—but don't assume all shelter dogs have problems; many just need a home.

A grown dog that has been mistreated, however, may require more time and patience from you than even a small puppy. It may also be set in its ways and accustomed to doing things differently from what you expect, and it may be hard work convincing it that you are now in charge. But if you don't want a puppy—or don't mind much either way—and you're willing to take into account the fact that an adult dog may have some socialization problems that you'll have to straighten out, you'll find a good friend in an adult dog.

Selecting Your Dog: The Do's And Don'ts

Let's assume you've decided to get a dog, and you have some idea about the kind of dog you'd

WELL-BRED DOGS

A brief guide to some of the most popular dogs in the seven purebred groups.

SPORTING DOGS

Brittany   *30-40 pounds.* Happy, alert, compact dog. Popular hunting dog.

Cocker Spaniel   *22-28 pounds.* Smallest sporting dog. Sturdy. Popular house dog. Affectionate and loyal. Requires grooming.

German Short-Haired Pointer   *45-70 pounds.* Good hunter. Easy to train. Good family pet. Does best in country rather than city.

Golden Retriever   *55-70 pounds.* Good hunter. Very intelligent. Used as guide dog for the blind. Great family dog that's excellent with children. Needs exercise.

Irish Setter   *50-70 pounds.* Very popular dog. Good sense of smell. Good hunter. Temperamental, but good with children.

Labrador Retriever   *55-75 pounds.* Very intelligent. Used as guide dog for the blind. Good hunter. Fine family pet and gentle with children. Needs exercise.

Springer Spaniel   *45-55 pounds.* Intelligent. Fast. Good bird hunter. Affectionate. Loyal family pet but somewhat stubborn. Needs exercise.

Weimaraner   *55-85 pounds.* Intelligent, affectionate animal. Good house dog but not terrific with children. Needs exercise.

HOUNDS

Basset Hound   *50 pounds.* Gentle, devoted animal. Good family pet. Does well in city. Stubborn, so is difficult to train.

Beagle   *20-30 pounds.* Good indoor and outdoor dog. Great for a family. Barks a lot. Stubborn, so is difficult to train.

Dachshund   *18-20 pounds.* Better with adults than children. Good house pet. Affectionate. Prone to back problems.

HERDING DOGS

Collie   *50-75 pounds.* Excellent family pet. Somewhat independent. Great with children. Requires regular grooming.

German Shepherd   *60-85 pounds.* Hardy. Intelligent. Good family pet. Good with children. Used as guide dog for the blind.

Old English Sheepdog   *75-90 pounds.* Excellent house dog but needs exercise. Requires considerable grooming and sheds heavily.

Shetland Sheepdog (Sheltie)   *16 pounds.* Good in limited space. Obedient. Good with children. Demands affection. Needs grooming.

WORKING DOGS

Akita   *80-100 pounds.* Very affectionate family dog. May be aggressive toward other dogs.

Alaskan Malamute   *50-90 pounds.* Great strength. Aggressive with other dogs. Not tolerant of young children. Requires exercise and regular grooming. Barks seldom. Very clean.

Boxer   *60-80 pounds.* Excellent family pet. Affectionate and playful. Needs plenty of exercise. Smooth, short-haired coat.

Doberman Pinscher   *60-75 pounds.* Good watch dog. Excellent family pet. Easy to train with firm discipline. Often is a one-owner dog; i.e., loyal to one family member.

Great Dane *120-150 pounds.* Good family dog. Affectionate. Good with children. Aggressive if threatened. Needs exercise.

Newfoundland *150 pounds.* Great family pet. Good with children. One of the sweetest-tempered of the large breeds. Intelligent. Fast learner.

Rottweiler *50-90 pounds.* Great protection dog with superb intelligence. May be aggressive toward people.

Siberian Husky *35-60 pounds.* Gentle, friendly, and good with children. Needs lots of outdoor exercise. Sheds heavily.

TERRIERS

Airedale *40-50 pounds.* Good house dog but independent. Good with children. Needs exercise.

Miniature Schnauzer *15 pounds.* Strong-willed and independent. Needs exercise. Fairly high-strung and not good with small children. Good watch dog. Needs grooming.

Scottish Terrier (Scottie) *17-21 pounds.* Great for apartment dwellers. Active. Intelligent. Not reliable around children.

West Highland White Terrier (Westi) *14-19 pounds.* Good family dog. Good with older children. Easy to groom.

TOYS

Chihuahua *1-6 pounds.* Smallest of all dogs. Intelligent. Easy to train. Friendly. Good house dog. Loyal. Good watchdog. Not good with small children.

Maltese *2-7 pounds.* Loyal. Intelligent. Excellent house dog. Good watchdog. Good with children. Needs grooming.

Pekingese *7-10 pounds.* Good, loyal pet. Very companionable. Independent and stubborn. Not good with children.

Pomeranian   *3-7 pounds.* Intelligent. Alert. Good house dog but not good with children.

Shih Tzu   *12-15 pounds.* Independent, but wonderful house dog. Great with children.

Yorkshire Terrier   *5-8 pounds.* Intelligent, high-spirited, and friendly. Very popular house dog. Good with children. Sheds little.

NON-SPORTING DOGS

Bichon Frise   *12-18 pounds.* Affectionate, playful. Needs attention.

Boston Terrier   *15-25 pounds.* Very good family pet. Somewhat intolerant of young children. Often needs Caesarean section for delivery of pups.

Bulldog   *40-50 pounds.* Wonderful family pet. Excellent with children and strangers. Needs little grooming. Has whelping problems and breathing problems.

Chow Chow   *50-60 pounds.* Only dog with blue-black tongue. Very powerful. Devoted family pet. Does not trust strangers.

Dalmatian   *50-55 pounds.* Very intelligent. Loyal house pet. Needs plenty of exercise. Best with older children.

Lhasa Apso   *15-16 pounds.* Beautiful small dog. Excellent house pet. Very independent. Difficult to train. Not always good with small children.

Poodle
Standard   *45-55 pounds.*
Miniature   *16 pounds.*
Toy   *7 pounds.*
Intelligent, active, alert animal. Easily trained. Some miniatures and toys are too excitable to be suitable for families with young children, but standards are very good with children. Sheds little, but requires a lot of coat care, including clipping.

like to share your home with. You're ready to buy your dog, but don't rush into it. Here, as elsewhere, impulse buying can get you into a lot of trouble. Where you get the dog from is as important as the sort of dog you get. If you're looking for a purebred dog, go to breed shows and talk to owners. Buy dog magazines and study them, or go to the library and read up on the different breeds. Look on bulletin boards in grocery stores. Check the advertisements in your local newspapers. Ask around. Call the local veterinarians. Very often a veterinarian will know of dogs that are available for sale or adoption. Visit humane shelters and observe the physical environment (it should be clean and pleasant) and the condition of the animals.

You can acquire a dog from one of several sources, the most common being a private owner, a breeding kennel, or a shelter or humane society. Whichever source you choose, certain basic rules and safeguards apply, and there are signs that can alert you to the fact that the source is less than reputable. You won't go far wrong if you keep in mind the do's and don'ts:

• *Don't* buy a puppy before it's six weeks old—the ideal age is eight weeks. Puppies that are removed from the litter too soon often develop strong attachments to people but don't get along with other dogs. Conversely, the longer a puppy is deprived of affectionate human contact, the longer it'll take to adjust to people later on.

• *Don't* buy from any establishment that is not clean and orderly, or where the dogs seem listless and out of condition. Unsanitary surroundings breed unhealthy puppies.

• ***Don't*** buy from a "puppy mill"—a place that's full of puppies of many different breeds.

• ***Don't*** buy from any owner who won't let you come into the house to inspect the dog, or won't let you spend time alone with the dog.

• ***Don't*** buy from any owner who seems reluctant to answer your questions or provide a detailed medical history of the dog.

• ***Don't*** accept a dog from an owner who won't give you an unconditional guarantee that, if your veterinarian finds something wrong with the dog in the first two or three days after purchase, you can return the dog for a full refund.

• ***Don't*** believe anyone who tells you that a puppy under four months old has had "all its shots." It can't be true.

• And when you're choosing from a litter of puppies, ***don't*** choose the one that's shivering in a corner—even if you feel sorry for it. It's the "runt," or weakest of the litter, and it may never grow into a really healthy dog.

• ***Don't*** accept a puppy that has diarrhea; it can be the sign of internal parasites or other health problems.

• ***Do*** check on the reputation of the establishment you're getting the dog from. Ask your veterinarian or, if you're buying a purebred, check with the

21

breed club for that type of dog. (Breed clubs are organizations of people with a special interest in one breed of dog, and they know all the main breeders in the country.) You can find the name and address of the breed club you're interested in from the American Kennel Club (AKC), which was established in 1884 as a nonprofit organization devoted to the advancement of purebred dogs. The AKC is made up of over 500 dog clubs throughout the United States. It maintains a registry of recognized breeds and enforces rules and regulations governing all dog shows under the Club's direction. You can write to the American Kennel Club at 51 Madison Avenue, New York, New York, 10010.

The United Kennel Club (UKC) maintains the second largest registry in the U.S. and registers a number of breeds not recognized by the AKC. The United Kennel Club is located at 100 E. Kilgore Road, Kalamazoo, Michigan, 49001.

• *Do*, if at all possible, observe a puppy's parents and check out their temperaments. Aggressive parents breed aggressive puppies. Although the environment you provide for the puppy will have a lot to do with molding its personality, seeing the parents will give you a 50 percent chance of predicting what to expect as the puppy grows up. If you're buying a purebred puppy, do be aware of any hereditary defects the breed is susceptible to— if you've done your homework, you'll know what they are. Ask the breeder if a veterinarian has checked the puppy for these defects.

• *Do* be impressed by the professional or home breeder who has these checks completed routinely before offering puppies for sale, and who encourages you to have the puppy examined by your veterinarian immediately after purchase. Any reputable breeder will give you the option of returning the dog if your veterinarian finds anything wrong in the early days.

• *Do* make sure, if you're buying a purebred dog, that the breeder gives you the necessary papers. When you buy a purebred dog that comes from AKC-registered parents, you should be given an AKC form filled out by the seller. When you complete this form and send in the proper fee, your dog will be registered also. It is the seller's responsibility to provide you with all the registration forms.

The breeder should also give you a copy of your dog's pedigree, or family tree. Note that a pedigree is, in itself, no guarantee that your purebred dog will do well in dog shows. Basically, all the pedigree tells you is that for three generations back the puppy comes from purebred stock.

A good breeder who knows you're buying the dog for show purposes will not, however, sell you a dog that doesn't show promise of becoming a good "show specimen." Breed clubs are closely knit enclaves where everyone knows everyone else, and the breeder's reputation is on the line. So it's clearly in the breeder's best interest to sell only puppies that will do credit to the kennel's name.

• If you're getting the dog for your family, *don't* hesitate to take the whole family along to see how the dog reacts. If you have young children, ask the owner how the dog gets along with children and how it reacts to a lot of excitement. Puppies usually love to play and bound around with children, but an older dog who has lived a quiet, sedate life around adults may have a hard time adjusting to a livelier environment.

• *Do* spend time alone with the dog you plan to buy. Take the puppy away from its littermates to see how it reacts—a well-adjusted puppy will enjoy the extra attention and fondling; a weak or very shy puppy will probably be undemonstrative and appear lethargic or overly timid, and maybe you'll want to choose a more sociable pup. If you're buying an adult dog, spend a few minutes with it away from its owner; this will give you a chance to estimate how willing the dog is to make friends with someone new. If it snarls or shrinks away from your friendly approach, it may have had bad experiences which will make for a difficult adjustment period. This opportunity to check each other out is particularly important when you're getting a dog from a shelter, since you have no knowledge of its parentage or past beyond what the shelter staffers can tell you from their own observations.

• Above all, *do* ask as many questions as you want. A reputable owner or breeder who's anxious to place an animal in a good home will be glad to answer all your queries. Any reluctance to answer questions or to let you see the environment is a sure sign that you'd do better to look elsewhere.

YOUR DOG BECOMES ONE OF THE FAMILY

You have now made some decisions about your dog; you know if you want a male or female, a purebred or a mutt, a puppy or an adult. You've looked into various sources and decided where to get your dog. Now's the time to do some practical preparation for dog ownership. Here's what you need to do before you bring the newcomer home:

• Brief the family on how to treat the newcomer.

• Arrange a sleeping place for the dog.

• Be prepared to provide appropriate food and water.

• Decide where the dog will urinate and defecate and, if the dog is not already trained, make plans for house-breaking.

• Buy a collar and leash if you're planning to take the dog out of the house right away.

• Check on local licensing requirements and regulations that affect dog owners.

• Locate and introduce yourself to a veterinarian.

The arrival of a new pet is always exciting, especially when there are children in the family, but too much action and emotion will disturb and confuse

the dog. Remind everyone that overexcitement will
panic the dog, that a puppy tires easily just like a
baby, and that a grown dog will need time to adjust
to a new environment. If you have children, remind them that you're not going to let them carry
the puppy around and display it to all their
friends—not at first, anyway. For one thing, an
animal is not a toy. For another, a puppy will
squirm a lot because it's insecure, and may squirm
right out of a child's arms and fall.

Remember, also, that in the dog's eyes, children
are not dominant family members—*you* are the
boss. So let the kids know that they are not to try
to discipline or train the puppy in the early days.
That's your job.

Where Will The Dog Sleep?

The sooner you introduce your new pet to its
sleeping quarters, the better off both of you are. If
the dog is a puppy, you need a place where you can
keep it confined until it is trained to be clean in the
house. One solution is a room with a gate—like a
child's safety gate—across the doorway. Since the
dog's going to be part of the family, this area of
confinement should be where there's lots of action;
the kitchen is a good place.

Put the dog's bed in the room you've chosen,
with a layer of papers nearby for it to use for urinating and defecating. Tell everyone that it's to be
allowed only in this one room until it's trained.

Sleeping in a confined space is very comforting
and dogs, like people, like to have a place of their
own. You can buy a dog bed for the newcomer, but

it's not strictly necessary. A box lined with a blanket or some of your old sweaters will work just as well. Besides, an article of your clothing will help it get used to your particular smell. Cut the sides of the box down so that it can get out easily.

Whatever sleeping arrangement you make for the dog, be sure that the bed is warm, easy to get in and out of, and out of drafts. Raise the bed off the floor a bit if drafts are a problem. The first few nights that a puppy spends away from the litter can be traumatic for it, and for you. It helps to tuck a hot water bottle into its bed and to set a ticking clock or a quietly playing radio nearby; these surrogates will take the place of the warmth and sounds of the litter and help it feel less lonely.

If the puppy cries the first few nights, be patient. Don't give in and let it sleep in your bedroom or on your bed; you'd be setting a precedent you may not be happy with later. After a few nights, it'll quiet down and be content in its own bed. The same goes for the older dog—although in this case you can dispense with the hot water bottle and the clock.

Crate training, which is recommended by professional trainers, provides puppies with a sense of security and privacy. Crates, or wire cages, are available at any pet supplier and usually are collapsible when not in use. The best type lets the dog see out on all four sides. Basically, the crate is like a baby's playpen, and it should be big enough for the dog to lie down and turn around, but small enough so that if it eliminates in the crate it will be soiling its own bed. The whole idea is that the puppy will not, or should not, relieve itself where it sleeps. If you choose to use a crate, remember these things:

• The cage must be large enough to accommodate the dog so that it can turn around and lie down comfortably.

• Line the bottom of the crate with a blanket or rug, and provide something to chew on and a couple toys.

• Remove your puppy's collar before placing it inside the crate to prevent the possibility of it getting caught and hurting the puppy.

• The puppy must sleep in the crate at night.

• Give the puppy an opportunity to relieve itself before it is put in the crate.

• During the first weeks, give your puppy a treat when it enters the crate so that it learns to associate good things with its little home. Stay near it and offer words of praise and encouragement.

• Begin your crate training schedule by putting your pet in the crate for small increments of time. Never let it out when it is barking. If the barking continues nonstop, the pet should be verbally reprimanded and then praised once it stops. Don't let it think that by barking it can get its way.

• Your puppy can be put in the crate for one- to two-hour periods at regular intervals throughout the day, probably during its nap time or when it will be left alone. A pet may be in a crate for an even longer amount of time while you're out of the house, but never for more than four hours at a time without the ability to relieve itself.

• Most puppies can begin to be "weaned" from their crate at five or six months of age. After that, pet owners should consider enrolling their puppies in obedience school.

• Crate training is not recommended for puppies that are left alone for long periods of time. A puppy that is isolated and denied companionship may become depressed or possibly destructive. Use the crate as a training tool; not as a way of life for your puppy or dog.

If you want your dog to live outside, you must provide suitable housing to protect it against extremes of heat or cold. When you're buying or building a doghouse or kennel, make sure that it meets the following requirements:

• It must be built above the ground, so that air can circulate underneath the structure and keep the floor dry.

• It must be big enough for the dog to move around in comfortably.

• It must be sheltered from direct sun or strong winds.

• Bedding—hay or wood shavings, for instance— must be changed frequently.

If you're also constructing a dog run—a place where the dog can exercise and also urinate and defecate—your main concerns are safety and sanitation. The run must be escapeproof with sides high enough to deter the dog from jumping out. And it must be easy to clean; gravel is fairly easy to maintain, and concrete flooring is the ideal solution because you can hose it off and disinfect it very easily. Grass or dirt runs cannot be cleaned effectively, and they can harbor the eggs of parasites like roundworms and hookworms for an indefinite length of time.

What Will The Newcomer Eat?

Feeding and nutrition requirements vary according to the age of the dog, and the charts in the next chapter give guidelines on nutrition for dogs of varying ages. When you adopt a grown dog, it's easy enough to follow the feeding schedule used by the previous owner. If you want to make changes in that schedule, do it gradually. If your veterinarian, in the course of his or her initial examination, feels that the dog has been getting an inadequate diet, he or she will make recommendations for a special diet.

Feeding a puppy takes a bit more work. Puppies are usually weaned—introduced to solid food—at four to five weeks old. By six to eight weeks, the mother is hardly nursing them at all, and she will encourage this independence by pushing them away when they try to nurse. So when you take an eight-week-old puppy home, it should be fully weaned and accustomed to solid food. You must, however, feed it at least three or four times a day, and it needs two or three times the calories that it'll need when it's fully grown. Remember, too, that any dog must have a supply of fresh water readily available at all times.

What About House-Breaking?

Training a dog to urinate and defecate only outdoors or in acceptable places is not difficult provided that everyone concerned with the dog understands the routine and follows it consistently.

If you are training a puppy in a single room or in a crate, place several layers of newspaper in one corner of the room, and put its food and water nearby. A young puppy needs to void urine or feces or both immediately after eating, so as soon as it's finished its food, pick it up and put it on or near the papers. When it uses the papers, make a big fuss and let it know that it's done the right thing. If you catch it in the act of voiding off the papers, pick it up immediately and put it on the papers.

When your puppy gets it right, praise it lavishly. Don't ever discipline if you don't actually see it making a mistake. An animal can't associate punishment with a past act. And be careful how you discipline when you're trying to housebreak a dog. A stern voice is all you need. If you're too rough, you'll end up with a dog that's scared all the time.

When the puppy is using the paper 100 percent of the time, it is ready to venture out of the confinement area. But even now, watch every move until you're quite sure it's not going to transfer its attention from the training papers to a corner of your best rug.

If you choose not to paper train, be prepared to spend a good deal of time taking the puppy out-

31

side. Immediately when it wakes from sleeping, take it out to the area you've designated for its use and set it down. If it voids, praise it and make a big fuss about how clever it is. If you take it out to the same place every two hours, it should soon get the idea of what you want it to do.

If you're outdoor training a puppy and keeping it in a cage between outings, don't be disturbed if it voids in the cage. You've probably heard that a dog will never soil its sleeping quarters, and this usually holds true for older dogs. But a young puppy can't hold its urine all night, and if it's confined in a cage it has no choice but to void right where it is.

Apart from when it wakes up and after eating, there's another time when a puppy may need to urinate and that's after it's been playing hard. Be aware of this and take it to its paper or outdoor spot as soon as the game is over.

Remember that your puppy is a social creature and wants to please you. So with patience, perseverance, and consistency on the part of you and your family members, house-breaking should be a fairly painless procedure for all involved regardless what method you use.

When you bring an older dog into your home, you'll need to approach training in a different way. Since the dog is used to other routines, paper training may be a difficult job—especially if the dog has never been trained at all. As with a puppy, you can try paper training or regular trips to the outside area designated for the dog's use. And, as with a younger dog, take the dog outside every two hours and praise it lavishly when it performs in the right place. If the older dog urinates or defecates in the house, scold it *only* when you catch it in the act. Don't rub its nose in any mess it makes; this may relieve your feelings of anger or frustration, but the dog learns nothing from it. Training your older dog may take as long, or even longer, than training a puppy, but the dog will eventually respond to your verbal encouragement and praise. Once it's trained, you'll only need to take it out two or three times a day.

One of your major responsibilities as a dog owner is to clean up after your dog. In some areas, you're legally required to do so. But even where no specific legal restrictions exist, common sense tells you that the health of your dog depends on the cleanliness of its surroundings. Parasites and germs are transferred in the feces, and if waste is not removed regularly, the dog will reinfect itself and infect other dogs.

If your dog uses your backyard or a dog run for voiding, try training it to use an area of concrete or some other hard surface rather than a grassy or overgrown area that cannot easily be washed down. Remove the feces immediately and get rid of them. The same applies if your dog voids off your property. It's your responsibility to remove the feces and dispose of them. This is particularly important in urban areas where there are heavy concentrations of dogs. Constant soiling of the ground in such areas makes for a year-round parasite problem.

There are a number of commercial "pooper-scoopers" on the market that you can use to remove your dog's feces. Some of these have long handles so you don't have to bend. Or you can use a small shovel and a plastic bag—it's just as effective. If every dog owner regularly cleaned up after its pet, the streets would be healthier and more pleasant for everyone, and there would be less hostility between people who own dogs and people who don't.

What About Leashes And Grooming Aids?

The type of basic grooming equipment you need—there's not much of it, in any case—depends on the type of dog you have. And you don't always have to buy it before you get the dog. Sooner or later, however, you will need these items:

Collar and leash. In many areas, particularly urban areas, you are legally required to keep your dog on a leash. If you have a larger dog, you will also need a chain choke collar. This is, as the name suggests, a chain that can be loosened or tightened as required. It's a valuable aid when you're obedience-training a dog, and it will restrain a large dog from taking you for a walk, rather than the other way around. The chain forms a collar, and if the dog lunges, the chain tightens automatically and restrains it. Always use a chain choke with care. If you're careless, you can, literally, choke the dog; at the very least, you can make it uncomfortable and cause it to cough. Let your veterinarian demonstrate how to use the chain and where it should, and should not, lie on the dog's neck. Buy a chain

choke collar that is one inch longer than the mea-
surement around the largest part of your dog's
neck.

Nail clippers. Unless a dog exercises enough on
hard ground to keep its nails worn down, you will
have to clip them. Use only clippers intended for
dogs, not those intended for people. Your veterinarian will recommend a brand, and detailed instructions for clipping a dog's nails are given in the
chapter on grooming.

Brush and comb. The length of the dog's coat
determines the type of brush and comb you'll use.
Refer to the section on grooming and the illustrations there to decide what's best for your dog.

The Legalities Of Owning A Dog

Besides being a good neighbor and doing everything possible to prevent your neighbor from
disliking your dog, you are obligated by certain
laws to carry out certain tasks. Most communities
have leash laws which require your dog never to be
off leash when outside your property. Many areas
require you to clean up your dog's feces, and in
certain cities dogs must eliminate only in the curb
of the street. These "scooper" laws are designed to
eliminate dog feces from public and private
grounds in order to control the transmission of
disease and prevent dogs from getting a reputation
as a nuisance. Rabies vaccinations are required by
law in every state of the United States, and most
areas also require that you license your dog. The
cost of the license frequently helps support the
local animal pound.

Unfortunately, all these laws were made necessary because irresponsible owners allowed their dogs to run loose and harass farm animals, wildlife, and people, and to soil lawns, gardens, and public parks. In fact, being a responsible pet owner requires very little effort beyond normal consideration for other people. You can call your local city hall or municipal building for information on requirements in your area.

You And The Veterinarian

As soon as you acquire a dog, you should have it checked out by a veterinarian. How do you locate a good veterinarian? First, ask your pet-owning friends—they're probably as familiar with their veterinarian as with their physician and chose him or her for the same reasons: professional competence, reasonable fees, convenience of hours and location, and genuine interest in his or her patients. If none of your friends are pet owners, call up the local veterinary association and ask for recommendations.

Once you've decided on a veterinarian, call up, introduce yourself, and arrange to visit the facility. Veterinarians, like doctors, are often very busy, but they are always happy to show you around.

What are you looking for in this initial visit to the veterinarian? Basically, you're checking out these points:

• **Is the facility clean, orderly, and pleasant?** A veterinarian's office should be as clean as your own doctor's office.

• **Is emergency service available?** If your dog gets sick or is involved in an accident out of office hours, what will you do? Many veterinarians belong to emergency clinics which function after their own hospital closes. Be sure that your veterinarian is a member of such a clinic, or has some other adequate emergency service available.

• **Is the veterinarian willing to answer all your questions?** A good veterinarian will be able to answer your questions in understandable terms—you and the veterinarian, after all, are partners in caring for your pet's health. Your veterinarian should also explain the fee scale for different services.

• **Are the two of you going to get along on a professional level?** It's important that you feel comfortable with the person who'll be caring for your pet. Lack of communication is one of the most common reasons that client and veterinarian part company.

Communication between client and veterinarian works both ways. Treat the veterinarian as you would your own doctor. Don't make unnecessary calls. Follow the veterinarian's instructions precisely. And, as you become a more experienced dog owner, use your judgement to decide what is an emergency and what isn't.

Your dog's first visit to the veterinarian's office should be within a few days of the new pet's arrival in your home. At this first visit, your veterinarian will give the dog a thorough physical examination, and, if the dog is a puppy, administer the

first of the series of vaccinations that are necessary
to protect the animal against a number of canine
diseases. At this time, the veterinarian will also
advise on diet and set up a future vaccination
schedule for the dog. Further information on vaccinations is given in a later chapter. If your dog is a
puppy, this first visit to the veterinarian should
take place between the ages of six and eight weeks.

Remember to take a sample of the dog's stool
along to the veterinarian's office. The stool will be
analyzed for parasites and, if necessary, a worming
schedule will be set up.

Elective Surgery

Your initial visit to the veterinarian with your
new pet is an appropriate time to discuss whether
or not to have the dog neutered. Apart from the
obvious advantage of avoiding accidental parent-
hood, both male and female animals can benefit
from neutering. The procedure reduces the incidence of certain health problems. Contrary to what
you may have heard, neutering does not have
adverse effects on the personality.

Neutering comes under the heading of "elective
surgery"—surgery that you choose to have done
even though it is not necessitated by any direct
health problem.

Neutering, or castrating, the male dog involves
the surgical removal of both testes from the scro-
tum. It is a simple procedure and presents few
problems. It's done in the veterinary hospital under
general anesthetic and the dog can usually go home
the next day. Most veterinarians advise that the

male dog should be neutered at six to nine months, although it is possible to neuter a healthy dog at any age.

Male dogs that are not neutered sometimes have a tendency to roam, and they may develop socially unacceptable habits such as "mounting" objects or people (that is, assuming the posture for mating), urinating on the furniture, or being very aggressive toward other male dogs. Neutering usually reduces or eliminates these bad habits.

It's not true that neutered dogs become fat, lazy, and unresponsive. Dogs get fat and lazy because they're over-fed and under-exercised, and an unresponsive dog is usually indicating that its owner is not giving it much incentive to respond.

The female dog's reproductive cycle—also known as the estrous or heat cycle—usually begins when she's about eight months old, when she comes into heat for the first time. (Note that giant breeds tend to come into heat later. The cycle should begin before the dog is a year old but sometimes doesn't start until 15 months.) There are exceptions, but most female dogs come into heat every six months. The normal heat or estrous cycle lasts about three weeks, and only in the second week is the dog capable of conceiving.

The first sign that the female dog is in heat is a swelling of the external genitalia (vulva), accompanied by slight bleeding from the vulva. If your dog leads an active social life, you'll notice that every male dog in the neighborhood is suddenly showing up to visit. In fact, since most female dogs are very fastidious about cleaning themselves when they're in heat, you may realize that your dog suddenly is surrounded by suitors before you notice the physical signs.

If you plan to breed the female dog, it's advisable to wait until the second heat because it gives her the chance to mature fully before having puppies. If you do not plan to breed her, it makes sense to have her spayed.

A female dog is made incapable of breeding by a surgical procedure called ovariohysterectomy, more commonly known as spaying. This involves the removal of the ovaries and the uterus; the female's heat periods stop and she cannot, of course, have puppies.

Ideally, the female dog should be spayed at about six months of age, when the procedure is simpler and recovery faster, although spaying can be done at any age with no lasting ill effects. Spaying while she's young significantly reduces the risk of breast cancer and prevents infection of the uterus (pyometra) and false pregnancy.

Spaying does alter the metabolism of the female dog to some extent, and she may put on weight unless her diet is controlled and she gets plenty of exercise. Avoiding this weight gain, however, is a simple matter, and spaying may even increase her life span.

Spaying is done under a general anesthetic. An incision is made in the abdomen, the ovaries and uterus are removed, and the incision is closed with stitches. The dog must be kept quiet for three to four days, and the stitches can usually be removed after 10 days.

Certain purebred dogs that are to be exhibited in dog shows must have their tails docked and/or their dewclaws removed in order to conform to breed standards set by the American Kennel Club. Unless this is done, they cannot be exhibited in AKC shows. Both procedures are carried out when the puppies are three to five days old, when both the discomfort to the pup and the aftercare necessary are minimal. Tail docking involves surgically cutting the tail at a joint. Among the purebreds required to have docked tails are Doberman pinschers, boxers, schnauzers, and poodles.

The dewclaws are the nails located on the inside of the front paws and occasionally on the rear paws; they are more or less equivalent to human thumbs, but (unlike human thumbs) serve no useful function. The dewclaws are removed at the same time that the tail is docked, and even if the procedure is not required by AKC breed standards, it's advisable to have it done—especially to working and hunting dogs whose dewclaws can catch and tear.

Both tail docking and dewclaw removal can be done when the dog is older, but the procedure is a lot more difficult at a later stage of development.

Some breeds are usually exhibited with their ears cut (cropped). Doberman pinschers, for instance, have naturally floppy ears that are frequently cropped to a pointed, upstanding, triangular shape. The same is true of miniature schnauzers and Great Danes. Ear cropping is a procedure that should be discussed with a veterinarian. If it is to be done, it should be done when the dog is eight

41

to 12 weeks old. Many countries, England and Canada among them, do not permit ear trimming, and Doberman pinschers, Great Danes, and other breeds are exhibited with their natural ears.

Saying Goodbye

Hard as it may be to think of—especially when you've just acquired a healthy young dog—one of the services your veterinarian may one day have to perform for you is euthanizing your pet. Dogs age faster than people and begin to fail much earlier. Often an aging dog will lose a lot of weight, want to sleep all day, or become disoriented. Some older dogs start to urinate and defecate in the house. Old age may also bring loss of sight or hearing. Watching an animal you love become debilitated through age or through chronic disease is one of the saddest parts of owning and caring for it.

How do you make that all too final decision to end the dog's life? When your pet can no longer function as a pet or lead a full, comfortable existence, it's time to make the decision to euthanize it. Although it's hard at the time, the decision to euthanize a dog that's either too old or too sick to go on living contentedly is one you cannot regret.

When the question arises, you should discuss it with all family members, including the children, and then with your veterinarian. In fact, the veterinarian is often the first one to realize the need to put the dog to sleep and to make the suggestion.

Euthanasia is a painless procedure in which a drug is injected into the dog. The drug simply acts first to put the dog to sleep, and then to stop the heart from beating. You may want to be with your dog while it's done.

Grieving

The loss of a pet causes its owner to feel the same grieving feelings as if a member of the family had died. Often it is difficult for a pet owner to express his or her feelings because it is often socially unacceptable to do so. Non-pet owners don't understand the attachment that developed and oftentimes belittle the strong feelings felt by the pet owner. Consequently, expressing grief externally is often not done, but it should be expressed.

The stages of grief for loss of a pet are identical for loss of a human loved one:

Denial. This is the first stage and involves the owner not admitting that his or her pet is dying or has died. This is a difficult stage to deal with since psychologists believe that denial occurs at the subconscious level.

Bargaining. In this stage, the pet owner, when faced with a terminally ill pet, promises never to discipline the pet again and will offer it the best food available, if only it will get better.

Anger. Anger is exhibited either at others or at one's self. The hostility exhibited to others, including the veterinarian, must be recognized for what it is. The condition will pass but must not anger others around the grieving pet owner. Self anger is manifested as guilt and is one of the most common phases of grieving. The pet owner feels it was his or her fault because he or she did something wrong to cause the pet to die or be sick.

Grief. This stage is the sad stage of grieving. This stage can lead to depression and altering of one's day-to-day activities. Psychologists agree that this is the stage that needs the most support. Grieving pet owners need to talk to someone about their feelings. If the feelings persist for a long time, or the pet owner feels severe depression, professional assistance may be necessary. Help can be obtained by contacting your veterinarian for guidance.

Resolution. This is the final stage of grieving. Since it is the acceptance stage of death, the pet owner is often ready to accept a new pet or at least give thought to the idea.

Pet Insurance

Medical care of pets is becoming very sophisticated. Dogs are living longer today than ever before thanks to medical advances that involve disease prevention and cure. Consequently, the costs of care have risen and it is not unusual for a dog with cancer to incur hundreds of dollars in medical costs to place it into remission. As a result, pet insurance companies have appeared on the scene. The cost of pet insurance is very reasonable, and although the insurance companies don't pay for everything, they pick up a large portion of the costs of most serious illnesses.

NUTRITION: HOW TO KEEP YOUR DOG WELL-FED

If you're around dog owners, you may hear them remark that the proverbial "dog's life" is actually a very comfortable life—all a dog has to do is eat, sleep, and play. And if you're a new dog owner, you certainly want to feed your dog right. The eating part of your dog's life, in fact, is the easiest part of your job. The commercial dog foods now available are easy to use and nutritionally sound. In fact, the increased life span of today's dog over its ancestors is partly due to balanced commercial products which contain all the fats, carbohydrates, essential amino acids, vitamins, and minerals that a normal, healthy dog needs.

Despite the availability of these foods, some pet owners still indulge a dog with tidbits, leftovers from the family table, and so on. The result? An overweight dog. Obesity is now a major problem among domestic animals, and obesity is the result of overfeeding or of spoiling the animal with table food instead of spoiling it with love and attention.

What kind of foods can you feed your dog? Basically, commercial dog foods come in three forms: dry, semi-moist, and canned.

Dry dog foods contain only six to 10 percent moisture. All the brands have basically the same content of vitamins, minerals, and essential amino acids, but the protein and fat content may vary. Most contain between 20 and 25 percent protein and about eight percent fat. Dry foods supply approximately 1300 to 1700 calories per pound of product.

Semi-moist foods usually come in sealed packages and supply about 1200 calories per pound of product. Most of these brands contain 23 to 40 percent moisture, 20 percent protein, and seven percent fat.

Canned dog foods contain a high percentage of moisture—70 to 80 percent. They usually provide about 600 to 700 calories per one-pound can, and have a protein content of 10 to 12 percent and a fat content of about six percent. If you're buying a canned food, check the label to make sure that it's marked as a "complete" diet.

The following nutrition guide gives an approximation of how much food a healthy dog will need at different stages of development. Quantities are given according to body weight. Note that these amounts apply only to healthy dogs living in a normal domestic environment. Working dogs, sick or debilitated dogs, some puppies, and pregnant dogs all have specific dietary requirements and should be fed according to the recommendations of a veterinarian.

Nutrition: The Well-Fed Dog

An active adult dog needs about 25 calories per day per pound of body weight. For example, if your active adult dog weighs 40 lbs., it needs 40 lbs. × 25 calories = 1000 calories a day. This is equivalent to about 2¾ to three cups of dry food.

Your 40-lb. house dog, though, needs only about 15 calories per day per pound of weight—
$40 \times 15 = 600$, or two cups of dry food.

If your 40-lb. dog is older or on a diet, it may need only 10 calories per day per pound.
$40 \times 10 = 400$ calories, or 1½ cups of dry food.

A puppy needs about 60 calories per day per pound of body weight, then that need decreases fairly rapidly until one year of age when it needs only about 25 calories per day per pound.

Use the charts on pages 48 and 53 to estimate how many calories your puppy or adult dog needs daily. It's important to remember, however, that dogs (like people) vary in appetite. These guidelines should be adjusted to the needs of the particular dog.

In order to use these charts, you must know the calorie content per cup, package, or can of product you are feeding. This information should be available on the package or from the manufacturer. As a guide:

1 cup of dry food = 300 calories
1 pkg. semi-moist food (6 oz.) = 400 calories
1 can dog food (16 oz.) = 600 calories

When treats are used, food intake should be reduced to make up for the calories these snacks contain.

Feeding A Puppy

When you take an eight-week-old puppy home, it should be completely weaned. Weaning (giving solid food) starts when the pup is four to five weeks old, and by six to eight weeks it's not nursing anymore. Up to the age of four to six months, the puppy needs approximately 60 calories a day for every pound of its weight. After six months, there's a fairly rapid decrease in its calorie requirements. And by the time it's a year old, it will need only about 25 to 35 calories per pound of body weight. Remember, however, that different breeds have different rates of growth and thus require different amounts of food.

Your eight-week-old puppy must be fed at least three or four times a day. When it starts losing interest in a meal, decrease the number of feedings so that—in the case of most types of dogs—by

DAILY CALORIE REQUIREMENTS FOR PUPPIES

Weight		Age					
		6 weeks	3 months	4 months	6 months	8 months	1 year
kgs.	**lbs.**	Calories Per Day					
2.3	5	525	395	305	265	200	175
4.5	10	1050	790	610	530	400	350
9.1	20	2100	1580	1220	1060	800	700
13.6	30		2370	1830	1590	1200	1150
18.2	40			2440	2120	1600	1400
22.7	50			3050	2650	2000	1750

•These figures are based on the results of scientific studies on dog nutrition.
•Note that a puppy's daily calorie needs decrease as it gets older.
•Breed of dog may cause variations..

eight months it's eating twice a day. Exceptions to this two-meal-a-day rule are some of the giant breeds, which may require multiple feedings up to and past one year of age. You will be talking to your veterinarian at intervals during this first year, and you will be advised on how many feedings your larger dog needs.

When you bring your puppy home, start it on a regular feeding schedule right away; this means feeding at the same times each day. In the first days, stay with the type of food the puppy was weaned on—ideally, this should be a good commercial dry puppy food. You can moisten the dry food with water to stimulate the puppy's appetite, but don't make it too soupy. An exception to this may be a very small puppy whose teeth are erupting late and who seems able to handle only moistened food. Remember to keep your dog supplied with fresh water at all times. Don't ever deprive the dog of water as a method of training.

Establishing Good Eating Habits

The amount you feed will vary from one dog to another. As a rule of thumb, follow the manufacturer's recommendations and cut the amount by one-third. Leave the food bowl down for no longer than 10 to 15 minutes. When the puppy walks away, assume it's had enough and pick the food up. If it gobbles up the food and looks around for more, give it some more. If the puppy walks away from the bowl without eating, don't assume that it doesn't like the cuisine and offer it something else. Remember that you're the boss and you set the schedule. If it rejects the food when you put it down, remove it until the next meal. Don't give in if it looks hungry 10 minutes later, and don't offer it table food—this will just establish lifelong bad habits and let it know that it can manipulate you to feed it on demand. Make it clear that if it doesn't eat on schedule, it can go hungry. A healthy puppy will soon learn that it'd better eat when food is offered rather than suffer those hunger pangs. You can make it easier on yourself by feeding the puppy at the same time that you eat and not offering it table food.

Should you give your puppy vitamins? As a rule, the answer is no. Vitamins are not usually necessary if the puppy is getting a balanced, high-quality diet.

A word of warning: Despite what you may have heard, rapidly growing large breeds do not need additional calcium and phosphorus provided they are getting a balanced daily diet. Your veterinarian can tell you that a lot of the bone problems seen in veterinary practice are due to over-supplementation of calcium, phosphorus, and vitamin D.

Do remember that for most breeds of dogs, the most rapid growth occurs in the first six months, and adequate nutrition during this time is essential to healthy development. Of course, the pup continues to grow after six months, but the rate of growth is slower and its nutritional requirements slow down.

Feeding The Adult Dog

Once your dog is fully grown, it usually does very well on two meals a day unless it belongs to one of the large, deep-chested breeds like the St.

TOXIC PLANTS

Algerian Ivy	Daffodil	Marijuana
Amaryllis	Dieffenbachia	Mistletoe
Arrowhead Vine	(dumbcane,	Philodendron
Asparagus Fern	mother-in-law	(heart leaf)
Avocado	plant)	Poppy
Azalea	Dracaena Palm	Pothos
Bird of Paradise	Elephant Ears	(devil's ivy)
Boston Ivy	English Holly	Schefflera
Caladium	English Ivy	Snow-on-the-
Calla Lily	Hydrangea	Mountain
Castor Bean	Iris	Spathiphyllum
Christmas Rose	Japanese Yew	Spider Plant
Chrysanthemum	Jerusalem	Tulip
Corn Plant	Cherry	Weeping Fig
Crown of	Lily of the	(ficus)
Thorns	Valley	

Bernard or Great Dane. If they eat too much at one time, these dogs can develop bloat—an accumulation of gas in the stomach which puts severe pressure on the internal organs.

If you're feeding your dog twice a day, the most convenient times are probably your breakfast and dinner times. The time you feed, however, depends on your convenience and your personal schedule. Don't ever succumb to that hungry look in your dog's eyes (it's faking) and give table scraps. You can end up with a fat dog or a dog with stomach and intestinal problems.

The quantity you feed a grown dog depends

51

partly on its activity level. A dog that lies around the house most of the day may need up to 30 percent fewer calories than a very active dog.

The diet for the adult dog is very similar to that of the puppy—a good-quality dry, semi-moist, or canned dog food. A sensible general rule is to take the manufacturer's recommended quantity according to the body weight of your dog, then reduce that quantity by about 30 percent. But use your common sense. If your dog is gaining weight, decrease the quantity of food. If it's losing weight, increase it. Remember, however, that a dog that's a bit hungry is healthier than one that's so full it can't walk away from its bowl.

What about supplements to your dog's basic diet? Adding a good-quality vegetable oil to its food provides fatty acids to the skin and prevents drying of the coat. Add one teaspoonful of oil for each 10 pounds of the dog's weight up to a maximum of two tablespoons. If the oil makes the dog's stool loose, discontinue it and ask your veterinarian for a supplement to give instead.

It's okay to give your dog an occasional treat between meals, but give only dog treats and remember that they have calories. A dog that's getting too many treats in addition to its regular diet will soon put on weight. Raw carrots make excellent treats and contain very few calories.

Contrary to what you may have been told, dogs don't need bones. Your dog's wild ancestors gnawed on bones because they needed the minerals that bones contain. A well-balanced commercial dog food already contains all the necessary miner-

DAILY CALORIE REQUIREMENTS FOR ADULT DOGS

Weight		
kgs.	lbs.	Calories Per Day
2.3	5	125
4.5	10	250
9.1	20	500
13.6	30	750
18.2	40	1000
22.7	50	1250
27.3	60	1500
31.8	70	1750
36.4	80	1800
40.9	90	1850
45.5	100	1900

• These figures are based on the results of scientific studies on dog nutrition.

• Active or working dogs may require 40 to 50% more calories than this chart depicts. Outside dogs and pregnant or lactating dogs need 30 to 50% more calories.

• The larger the dog, the fewer the daily calories required. For large breeds (breeds weighing more than 70 lbs. adult weight), reduce the above figures by 10%.

als. Feeding bones to your dog is asking for trouble; bones can cause constipation, intestinal obstruction, and broken teeth. It's also a fallacy that chewing on bones is necessary to keep the dog's teeth clean and healthy. If you want to give it something to chew on, choose a hard rubber toy or a rawhide or synthetic bone.

Feeding An Aging Dog

As your dog ages, all its functions slow down. It sleeps more and takes less exercise. Its kidneys begin to scar up and become unable to handle excessive protein. At this stage, you need to adjust the dog's diet by decreasing the amount of protein but increasing its quality. This can be accomplished by cutting down on dog treats, which frequently contain poor-quality protein.

If your dog develops heart disease as it gets older, a low-salt diet is indicated. Other disorders such as kidney disease, liver disease, or intestinal and stomach problems all require special dietary adaptations. As a rule, you should have your veterinarian recommend a suitable diet for an aging dog on the basis of the dog's general health.

If your veterinarian recommends a special diet, he or she will probably direct you to one of the commercially prepared foods that can be purchased only through a veterinarian. These are a bit more expensive than regular dog foods because they call for more expensive ingredients. A special diet formulated for dogs with food allergies, for instance, is made up of lamb and rice plus the necessary vitamins and minerals. The lamb adds to the expense, but it's used because very few dogs are allergic to lamb. You can make up a special diet for your dog at home, according to the veterinarian's recommendations, but you'll probably discover that the cost is no less than that of a commercial special food.

THE WELL-BEHAVED DOG

The well-behaved dog needs to learn more than just to be clean in the house. As your companion, your dog will go places and meet people with you, and you will expect it to behave in a socially acceptable way on these occasions. Training your dog to be a pleasure to have around can begin, in small but practical ways, as soon as it becomes part of your family. Later, you may decide you want to take it to obedience training classes. If your dog is a puppy, however, obedience classes should wait until it's at least six months old. Although there are some puppy classes available, most will not accept a dog under the age of six months. Like small children, puppies have a short attention span and are too busy playing to be bothered with appropriate behavior. Puppy classes are aimed at training the puppy to socialize with other dogs.

All the same, you can prepare your puppy for training even when it's small by introducing it to the commands you'll expect it to obey when it's older, and by using a firm voice and consistent behavior to get it accustomed to what you expect from it. For instance, you can call the pup's name and say "come." It's best to do this when you know it wants to come to you anyway, so that you can reinforce its good behavior by praising it. The full message may not get to it right away, but you're laying the groundwork for future obedience training.

Obedience:
More Than Cute Tricks

Some dog owners think it's cute to teach their dogs to roll over, sit up and beg, fetch the newspaper, or do other tricks. But that's not what obedience training is about. Obedience training teaches the dog to listen to your command, to obey when the command is given, and then to wait for the next command. Take an untrained, exuberant dog for a walk and it may try to pull you across a busy road against the lights. But if your dog is properly trained, it will obey your order to halt and sit at the curb and will then cross the street politely at your side when you give the command—a gentle pull at the leash is often enough.

There are many practical advantages of obedience training. A trained dog won't jump all over strangers (you may think it's okay to have it jump up, but not everyone likes dogs); it won't bark unnecessarily and infuriate the neighbors; it won't trample over other people's yards and chase their cats. It may well want to do all those things, but your command will stop it.

And, of course, training your dog is an important safety measure as well as a social one. A dog that's not trained to behave on busy streets is likely to end up the victim of a road accident.

If you have a very receptive dog, you may be able to train it quite adequately yourself, perhaps with the help of an instruction manual. Usually, however, you'll get better results from taking the dog to obedience classes. Moreover, you'll enjoy the classes, too—they're inexpensive, they're fun, they're rewarding, and you get to see how other people and their dogs get along.

Most beginning obedience classes run for 10 or 12 weeks and require your presence with your dog one night a week. Between classes, you're expected to practice with the dog at home. Your dog should learn to perform basic tasks calmly at the first command—to sit, stay, walk at heel, come on command, and so on. You can ask your veterinarian to recommend a class, or look for advertisements in the local newspaper. Remember, however, that the only right way to train a dog is with firm, consistent, and gentle handling. Harsh punishment is never appropriate, and you should never let your dog be part of any class where you feel that the trainer is mistreating the animals or encouraging training methods other than those based on kindness.

A word here on formal training, such as that undergone by dogs that work for a living as guard dogs, police dogs, or guide dogs for the blind. Training for all these animals is carried out by professionals and is a far more lengthy and involved process than that of obedience training a family dog. Police dogs and guide dogs are generally trained by, or in close cooperation with, the person who will handle them after training. Guard dogs are usually left at a facility for training, then the owner is in turn trained how to handle the dog. Although your dog may do a good job of protecting your property by barking at intruders or intimidating them by its presence, it is not usually wise to expect a professionally trained guard dog to double as a family pet.

The Well-Traveled Dog

A dog that has been obedience trained probably makes a better traveling companion than an untrained dog, and most owners travel with their dogs at some time or another—even if it's only to the veterinarian's office or to the grooming establishment for trimming or bathing. In fact, both of these trips are surefire anxiety producers for the dog and, if it doesn't particularly care for being in the car anyway, you're in for a miserable trip. Dogs that are inexperienced travelers frequently suffer from motion sickness which makes them drool or vomit; this is more frequently true of younger animals, but it does occur in adult dogs, too. You can, however, take practical steps while the dog is still young or a newcomer in your home to forestall motion sickness. Here's a simple program for getting your dog used to the car:

• Sit in your parked car with your dog for a few minutes each day. Talk to your dog to make it feel comfortable, but don't start the car.

• After a couple of days, repeat the procedure but start up the car. Don't drive anywhere; just praise the dog.

• After a few more days, put the dog where you want it to sit while traveling (in the back seat, for instance), start up the car, and drive around the block. If possible, go to a park or some other setting that will help the dog associate car travel with a pleasant outcome.

• Repeat this drill daily, increasing the distance you drive each day. With any luck at all, your dog will soon be acting like a seasoned traveler.

If these tactics don't work and your dog is consistently car sick, ask the veterinarian to prescribe medication for the dog before you take a trip.

There are several other important considerations to keep in mind when you take your dog in the car:

• Never let your dog sit on your lap while you're driving, and make sure large dogs stay in the back seat.

• Never let your dog hang its head out of the car window while the car's moving; the air blowing against its eyes can cause conjunctivitis (severe irritation of the tissue around the eyes). The dog's head and body may also be injured or crushed if there is a car accident.

• Never leave a dog unattended in a closed car on a hot day. The most common cause of heat prostration (often fatal) in dogs is overheating in an automobile. If you must leave the dog in the car, park the car in the shade and leave the windows partially open. However, don't leave the dog unless it's absolutely necessary; an excited dog in a closed hot car can overheat in just a few minutes and brain damage follows very quickly.

Air Travel: Checking Regulations

Specific regulations apply to dogs traveling by air

or on other forms of public transportation, and you should always check these out before a trip. Airlines require that the dog be enclosed in a travel kennel or crate. If the crate is small enough to go under your seat in the aircraft, the dog can travel with you; otherwise, the animal must travel in the baggage compartment. The baggage compartment is pressurized and the temperature controlled, so your dog will come to no harm (beyond, probably, being lonely and somewhat apprehensive).

Most airlines sell dog crates, and all you need to do is make sure that the crate is large enough for your dog to stand, turn, and lie down comfortably. Attach identification both to the crate and to the dog's collar, and attach to the crate copies of any health certification required by the state or foreign country to which the dog is traveling.

Your veterinarian can tell you what certification you need if you're taking your dog out of state, and be sure to get this information well ahead of time especially if you're traveling to a foreign country. In this case, contact the consulate for that country and have them send you the appropriate forms. Frequently, your state's Department of Agriculture will have to approve the documents—another good reason for not leaving it until the last minute.

Wherever you're traveling, take your dog to the veterinarian at least two weeks before your departure date. The veterinarian will make sure all of the dog's vaccinations are up to date, review the dog's medical condition, and, in some cases, prescribe a tranquilizer to calm the dog and counteract motion sickness.

Vacationing With Your Dog

It's quite possible to take your dog on vacation with you, but it requires both common sense and advance planning. First of all, be sure that the place you plan to stay at won't turn you away when you arrive with a dog in tow. Some hotel or motel chains publish directories listing which of their facilities allow dogs. Call the facility nearest to your home for information. Your local library is also a useful source of information. If you plan to camp, check on the regulations that apply at the campgrounds you wish to stay at. Again, you can get this information from directories available in most public libraries, or direct from the campgrounds.

Remember that the change of environment and general excitement of vacation time may affect a dog in unexpected ways. Your normally well-behaved dog may become a noisy, nervous problem and this will not only wreck your vacation but make you unpopular with others at your motel or campground. You can minimize these adjustment problems by taking along familiar objects like the dog's food dish, bedding, or toys; giving it lots of reassurance; and discouraging strangers who are over-eager to pet it. If you are not confident that your dog can handle a vacation away from home, it's best to make arrangements for its care and leave it behind.

The Stay-At-Home Dog

If, for one reason or another, it's not possible to take your dog with you on a trip, you have the options of either having the dog cared for in your own home, sending it to a boarding kennel, or (if the dog is adaptable) having it stay with a friend or neighbor it knows well.

In many urban areas, it's possible to find "dog sitters" who will care for the dog in your home. Your veterinarian may be able to recommend someone, or sitters may advertise in the local press. If the sitter is someone you don't know, be sure to check references.

If you decide to board your dog in a kennel, get recommendations from your friends or the veterinarian and, if possible, visit several kennels before you make your choice. Look for cleanliness and a caring staff, and don't patronize any kennel that seems reluctant to have you tour the facility— reputable establishments are always happy to show you around. The American Boarding Kennels Association (ABKA) makes available a list of member establishments along with advice on how to select a boarding kennel. You can write to the ABKA at 4575 Galley #400A, Colorado Springs, Colorado 80915. Once you've decided on a boarding kennel, make the reservation as early as possible—good kennels fill up fast, especially at vacation time.

Before you leave your pet in the care of anyone—friend or professional—make sure the person is fully aware of the animal's feeding schedule, habits, fears, idiosyncrasies, and so on. Make sure the dog's vaccinations are current, and leave the phone numbers of your veterinarian and emergency service. Then you can enjoy your trip with the confidence that your dog will be well cared for in your absence.

GROOMING: THE GOOD-LOOKING DOG

Good grooming is as important to your dog as it is to you. A well-groomed dog looks good and feels good, and grooming sessions serve two useful purposes beyond the obvious goal of cleanliness: They are (or should be) fun for you both, and they give you a chance to do a quick check on your dog's general health.

Grooming involves caring not only for the dog's coat, but also for the eyes, ears, nails, and anal sacs. The amount of grooming your dog needs depends a lot on the breed—and you'll have taken this into account before you took the dog into your home.

Combing and brushing are the first steps to keeping your dog well groomed. Combing separates the tangled hair at skin level; brushing removes dead hair and gives luster to the coat. Long-haired dogs like poodles, Yorkshire terriers, Maltese terriers, Lhasa apsos, Old English sheepdogs, and so on need to be combed and brushed frequently, sometimes every day, to prevent the hair from becoming matted. And the longer the hair, the more work it is for you. A short-haired dog usually won't need combing at all because the hair doesn't often tangle or mat. For these dogs, a good brushing is adequate.

Not all dogs take kindly to the grooming process,

but most of them love the attention and the good feeling they get from being groomed. And the best way to insure that grooming is fun for you both is to start with short, daily sessions when the dog is a puppy. The easiest way to groom a puppy or a small dog is on a table, so that you won't have to stoop. Just being on a raised surface will probably make the dog a bit nervous, so it'll stay still instead of bouncing around and complicating things. A slippery surface, though, may upset it thoroughly and is dangerous because the dog may skid and fall. Put a rubber mat on the table to give it a good footing.

Make the first grooming sessions short—just a few minutes a day—and heap your dog with praise at the end of each successful session. Tell the dog how proud you are of it and how beautiful it looks. Pretty soon it'll be looking forward to grooming sessions and the approval that accompanies them. Don't give up if your early attempts to groom your puppy are frustrating. Stick with it, take it slowly, and don't lose your temper.

As your dog gets used to being groomed, make sure that you handle all parts of its body during the process. Look at its eyes and ears; open its mouth and run your fingers along its gums. This way the dog will get used to your touch and you'll have a much easier job when the time comes to give it medication or inspect or clean its teeth.

If you happen to have a dog that—despite all your care and approval—hates to be touched, you'll have to use different tactics. You may need to recruit another family member to hold the dog

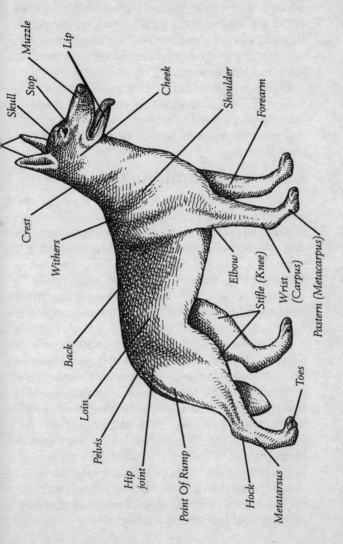

Skull, Stop, Muzzle, Lip, Cheek, Shoulder, Forearm, Crest, Withers, Elbow, Stifle (Knee), Wrist (Carpus), Pastern (Metacarpus), Back, Loin, Pelvis, Hip joint, Point Of Rump, Hock, Metatarsus, Toes

while you groom it. You may even have to restrain the dog with a muzzle. Don't let up on the praise, though, when it does behave. You don't often come across a dog that can't be persuaded to at least tolerate being groomed.

If, however, you do find that you've become the owner of a dog that won't let you groom it adequately, you'll need to rely on professional care. Ask your veterinarian to recommend a grooming establishment.

Grooming Equipment

The following equipment should be all you need to keep your dog looking good.

Brush and comb. If you've got a short-haired dog, use a medium soft brush to keep its coat in shape. The dog will find it very comforting, too, provided you remember always to brush in the direction of growth. With a long-haired dog you'll need to use first a comb to separate the tangled hair, then a firm bristle brush.

It's important to choose the right brush, and the best kind for all-around use is a soft wire slicker brush which is between the very soft brushes used on show dogs and the harsh slicker brushes sold in many pet stores. Natural bristle brushes are good, but they don't remove the dead hair nearly as effectively as the slicker brush. If the dog's coat is badly matted, a Universal brush (like a slicker brush but convex in shape) removes the mats much better than a slicker brush. When you're buying a comb for your dog, choose one that has half fine and half coarse teeth.

Scissors. With some breeds, such as poodles and Lhasa apsos, you'll need scissors to trim away hair around the eyes so that it won't get in the eyes and cause irritation or trap debris that could lead to an infection. You'll also use the scissors to cut away any hair that becomes matted around the rectum. Here, too, matted hair can collect debris and cause irritation or infection.

Nail clippers. It's very important to trim the nails of any dog that doesn't get enough exercise to keep the nails worn down naturally. Don't ever use human nail clippers on your dog. You can get special dog nail clippers from any pet supplier.

Shampoo. Your grooming supplies should include a special dog shampoo. Most human shampoos are much too harsh for a dog's skin. Don't think you're doing your dog a favor, either, by randomly using a product that also kills fleas. Again, these products are very drying and should be used only for the stated purpose—on a dog that has fleas—and on the advice of your veterinarian.

Miscellaneous supplies. Your grooming kit can usefully include a number of other items, many of which you may already have in your home: mineral oil (a drop in each eye before bathing prevents eye irritation); cotton swabs and baby oil for cleaning the ears; a commercial eyewash to use in the case of simple eye irritations; a child's toothbrush and either dog toothpaste or baking soda—dogs need their teeth cleaned, too; and styptic powder for bleeding nails.

Once you've got your dog accustomed to—and looking forward to—being groomed, you'll proba-

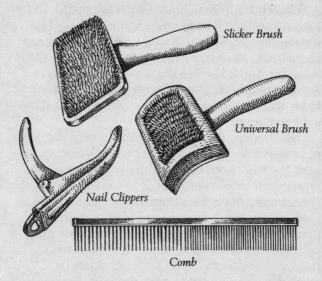

Slicker Brush

Universal Brush

Nail Clippers

Comb

bly need to groom it three or four times a week.
Start with brushing and combing. With a short-
haired dog, a brushing is all that's needed. Brush
firmly but gently, always following the direction of
the hair growth.

A long-haired dog will usually need combing
before you brush it; some breeds, like the Afghan
hound or Yorkshire terrier, will require daily attention. Use the comb to separate the tangled hair,
and comb a little at a time. Always comb from the
skin out, because the mats form at skin level. Don't
try to cut off a particularly stubborn mat; you'll
almost certainly end up cutting the skin. If it's
impossible to tease the mat apart, a bit at a time,
then you should probably seek professional help.

One advantage of regular grooming is that it cuts

down on the amount of loose hair you'll have to vacuum off the rug or the sofa. Certain breeds like German shepherds, Norwegian elkhounds, collies, and Pomeranians have a double coat. The under-coat is very soft and tends to trap loose hair, so regular (preferably daily) brushing with a stiff brush will remove this loose hair and keep it off your clothes and furniture.

Bathing: When And When Not To Bathe A Dog

It should not be necessary to bathe your dog more than once a month. A short-haired dog that leads a conservative indoor life won't need bathing even that often. Too frequent bathing is not only unnecessary but inadvisable—it robs the skin of its natural protective oils and causes it to become dry and scaly.

Don't make the mistake of bathing your dog just because "it smells." Dogs are supposed to have an odor—though not an offensive one—and any unusually noticeable odor may mean something quite different from straight-forward grubbiness. If there's a strong odor coming from your dog, check the mouth, ears, and anal sacs. Dental problems can cause a strong odor. Ear infections give off a musty smell which is immediately recognizable once you know what you're looking for. A strong, persistent odor coming from the anal sacs can indicate an infection. Don't bathe your dog to cover up any of these odors; they all require specialized treatment or veterinary attention.

If you've decided that your dog does need a bath, make sure you've got room to do the job. The bathtub is fine for most smaller dogs. A rubber mat in the tub will stop the animal from slipping around and getting panicky. If you've got a very large dog, your best bet may be to bathe it in the backyard and get the shampoo off with the garden hose. In this case, choose a warm, sunny day so that the dog will not get chilled by the cold water from the hose and will dry off quickly in the sun. If you're bathing the dog indoors, use lukewarm water and fill the bathtub or other container to the level of the dog's elbows. An alternative method is to use a shower hose attached to the faucet.

Before putting the dog into the water, make sure all the knots and tangles are combed out of its coat. Place a drop of mineral oil in the inner corner of each eye (use a dropper) to protect against irritation from the soap. Wet the dog thoroughly and pour a small amount of the dog shampoo you're using down its back. Vigorously massage the shampoo down to the skin, taking care to wash under the tail, the legs, and the abdomen. Rinse the shampoo off thoroughly so that there's no soap residue to cause irritation later. Let the dog shake to get the excess water out of its coat (this is where it's a real advantage to do the whole thing out-doors), then towel it dry.

If the dog is small enough and can tolerate the noise, you can finish drying it with your hair dryer—the blow kind. This may, however, drive it crazy. If it will let you use a blow dryer, use the warm setting only.

When you're bathing your dog, you have the ideal opportunity for checking out the skin all over the body for any irritations or lesions that may need attention. At this time, check also for ticks and fleas. If you find them, deal with them as discussed in the chapter on parasites.

General Health Care At Grooming Time

Whether you're bathing your dog or just brushing and combing it, part of the grooming session should include attention to the eyes, ears, nails, teeth, and anal sacs. A healthy dog's eyes should always be bright and shining, with wide-open lids. Occasionally the eyes may seem mildly irritated, in which case you can apply a commercial, nonmedicated eyewash. When you're grooming the dog, gently wipe away any discharge that has accumulated in the corners of the eyes. If there's a green or yellow discharge, call your veterinarian. This is particularly important if the discharge is accompanied by redness of the eyes. Another cause for veterinary attention is excessive tearing; the veterinarian will check that the tear ducts are functioning properly.

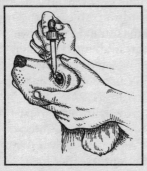

A drop of mineral oil in each eye prevents irritation from soap at bathtime.

White-haired dogs that tear a lot develop brown stains on the fur between the corners of the eyes and the mouth. Provided that the veterinarian has determined that the tearing is normal, there's nothing you can do about the discoloration.

Clean your dog's ears routinely, once a week. Cleaning is particularly important if the dog has floppy ears which keep the ear canal moist and prevent air circulation. This type of ear fosters the growth of bacteria and yeast, which are major causes of canine ear infections.

Clean the ears with a cotton swab dipped in baby oil. The long ear canal is L-shaped, going straight down and then turning in toward the head. At the end of the L is the eardrum. To clean the ear, hold the ear flap (or pinna) straight up above the head and gently place the swab into the canal in a vertical position; that is, facing down toward the floor. This way, the swab can't enter far enough into the canal to harm the eardrum.

Some dogs, like poodles, grow hair in their ears, and if this hair is not removed it can cause infection. Superficial hair can be removed easily: grasp it with your fingers and pluck it out. Deeper hair must be removed by a veterinarian, and so must any hair on an area of the ear which appears to be red or irritated. If there's an unpleasant odor from the dog's ears, or if it scratches at the ear or tilts its head persistently to one side, call the veterinarian.

Large domestic dogs that get plenty of energetic outdoor exercise usually wear down their nails naturally. Small dogs that spend most of their time indoors, however, need their nails cut. And shaggy dogs with long hair on their feet (like cocker spaniels) may deceive you into thinking their nails are not too long; look again.

Trimming a dog's nails is not as easy as it sounds. The process is simple, but the dog's reaction often turns it into a major production—it fidgets and complains so that it's hard for you to get the job done.

Before cutting the nails, look carefully to make sure you know what you're doing. Each nail has a blood vessel and a nerve—the quick. If you cut into the quick, you'll hurt the dog and cause bleeding. If the dog has white or pale nails, you can see the quick as the pink line running in the nail. Using the special dog nail clippers described earlier, cut the nail a little before the quick as shown in the illustration on page 74. If the dog's nails are black, your task is more difficult; clip a little at a time to be sure you don't cut into the quick. A generally safe rule is to cut just below the point where the nail starts to curve downwards.

If you accidently cut the quick, don't panic— although your dog will certainly complain. Apply a styptic powder or pencil to the cut, or apply direct pressure to the bleeding nail for five minutes.

When you're trimming the nails, don't forget to clip the dewclaws, which are equivalent to the nails on the human thumb. Some dogs have dewclaws on both front and back feet; some don't have any at all because they were removed when the dog was a puppy. These nails never touch the ground and have no chance to wear down.

Even conscientious owners often overlook the

care of their dog's teeth. If you have a puppy, watch for it to begin replacing its front baby teeth when it's three or four months old. At this time, you may see blood on the gums, empty spaces, or double teeth. It's unlikely that your puppy will have any teething problems, but occasionally the adult teeth come in before the baby teeth fall out. In this case, your veterinarian will correct the situation before the dog's bite (the way the top and bottom teeth close together) is affected.

The teeth of adult dogs often develop stains and dental calculus, commonly called tartar—the deposits located on the teeth at the gumline. If tartar

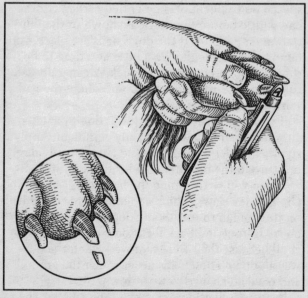

The correct way to clip a dog's nails

is allowed to accumulate, it will cause bacteria to form under the gum, and this will lead to pyorrhea (which is the accumulation of pus along the root of the tooth) and eventual tooth loss. Mouth odor is a sure sign of decay, infection, or a dietary problem, so any time your dog has "bad breath," have your veterinarian check it out.

Regular toothbrushing will do wonders to help keep your dog's mouth healthy. Use a child's toothbrush dipped in baking soda or dog tooth-paste and rub the teeth and gums vigorously. Do not use human toothpaste as it will upset your dog's stomach. There are many veterinary tooth-pastes on the market that will help greatly in reducing dental problems. Remember that a hard food diet and suitable toys to chew on—hard rubber or rawhide playthings, for instance—help somewhat to keep your dog's teeth in good shape. Do not, however, give a dog meat bones; they can splinter and injure the dog.

Care of the anal sacs should be part of every grooming. These sacs are located immediately under the rectum at the five o'clock and seven o'clock positions, and were originally used for marking out the dog's territory in the wild state. The odor of the material emitted from the anal sacs is very unpleasant. Normally, the sacs empty automatically each time the dog has a bowel move-ment, but variations in the diet and consequently in the consistency of the stool can impede this natural regulation.

By making sure the sacs are emptied regularly, you can avoid impaction, infection, and rectal irritation in the dog. To relieve blocked anal glands, take the dog's tail in one hand and raise it. Using a paper towel, place the index finger and thumb of your free hand over the five o'clock and seven o'clock positions respectively, and press the thumb and finger inward and then toward each other. This squeezes out the contents of the glands. Your dog will probably object to this procedure, so have someone hold its head while you do it.

Sometimes home treatment may not be effective, and a veterinarian has to squeeze the glands internally to empty them. If your dog is scooting (sitting with its tail extended and moving along the floor on its rear end) or showing other signs of discomfort that are not relieved by home treatment, take it to the veterinarian's office.

VACCINATION: A KEY TO GOOD HEALTH

Just as vaccinations now protect children from conditions that used to be killers, scientists have discovered ways to vaccinate dogs against a number of once fatal diseases. Vaccinations are a routine part of your preventive medicine schedule for your dog, and the first time you meet your veterinarian on a professional basis will probably be when you take your puppy for these shots.

Don't assume that because you plan for your dog to lead a sheltered life, it doesn't need to be vaccinated. Veterinarians hear this all too often and point out that a bigger myth couldn't exist. The best analogy is that of a bed-ridden person who lives alone and who never leaves the house, yet still gets sick. The viruses and bacteria that cause illness in both people and in dogs are easily spread either in the air or on shoes and clothing, and no dog is safe from diseases like canine distemper unless it has received the appropriate vaccination.

All puppies receive a certain amount of natural immunity to disease from their mother. The protective antibodies are passed to the puppies in the first milk—or colostrum—in the first 24 hours of life. This protection, however, is short-lived, depending in part on how well-protected the mother was before the birth of the litter. Some puppies

77

receive very little protection and are susceptible to disease as early as six to eight weeks after birth; most puppies lose all this acquired immunity by the time they are 14 to 16 weeks old. The veterinarian, therefore, starts vaccinating puppies when they're between six and eight weeks old. Your veterinarian will work out a suitable schedule for your particular dog, and the complete program will cover the following infectious diseases:

Distemper
Hepatitis (Canine Adenovirus Type-1/Type-2)
Leptospirosis
Parvovirus
Coronavirus
Canine Respiratory Disease (Kennel Cough)
Rabies

These diseases are explained below.

Distemper

Distemper is a highly contagious viral disease of dogs. Contrary to popular opinion, it has nothing to do with the dog's temperament or personality. It's caused by a virus, related to the human measles virus, that the dog contracts either by inhaling it from the air or by direct contact with an infected dog. The virus incubates in the dog for seven to nine days before any signs of the disease appear.

Signs and diagnosis. The first signs of distemper are commonly lethargy and an unusually high temperature—103° to 105°F. If the dog has no immunity to the disease, the virus infects the whole body causing a second rise in temperature along with signs of severe physical weakness, lack of appetite, discharge from the eyes and nose, cough, pneumonia, and—in many cases—diarrhea. Because these symptoms may also be indicative of other conditions, careful diagnosis is required. The veterinarian may take blood samples in order to make the diagnosis. The distemper virus also attacks the brain and can lead to convulsions and death.

Unfortunately, it sometimes happens that none of the early signs of distemper are recognized by the owner, and no action is taken until the dog shows signs of neurological damage—convulsions, jerking movements of the head and jaws, and inability to stand. If these occur, it may be necessary to euthanize the dog. If the dog survives, it may be left with permanent but acceptable neurological disturbances, like jerking movements of the head or legs. The dog, however, functions normally in every other way.

Treatment. Because distemper is caused by a virus, treatment is seldom effective. Occasionally, supportive therapy—good nursing care and careful feeding—and antibiotics for secondary infection will enable the dog to survive this very dangerous disease. Among other medications the veterinarian may prescribe are antidiarrheals, cough medicines, anti-convulsants, and intravenous fluids.

Prevention. If the female dog is properly vaccinated before she is bred, she will impart good temporary immunity to the puppies. The puppies must then be vaccinated at six to eight weeks, and twice more up to 16 weeks of age. Puppies must be kept away from older, unvaccinated dogs until the vaccination program is complete. Older dogs must receive booster shots each year in order to be fully protected. Remember that distemper is not just a "puppy disease"—it can affect dogs of all ages.

Hepatitis (Adenovirus Type 1 and Type 2)

Infectious hepatitis is usually caused by canine adenovirus type 1. The virus primarily affects the liver, and all members of the canine family are susceptible. It can affect dogs of any age but is most serious in the young. The virus is transmitted in the urine, stool, or saliva of an infected dog, and the incubation period before symptoms of the disease appear is six to nine days. Adenovirus type 2 is an important factor in kennel cough.

Signs and diagnosis. This disease can appear in many forms, but the most common signs are a rise in temperature (103°F/39°C to 105°F/40.5°C), lethargy, loss of appetite, tonsillitis, and possibly discharge from the eyes or nose similar to that seen with distemper. Very often the owner does not even realize the dog is sick until he or she notices a cloudiness in the cornea of one or both eyes; this condition is known as "blue eye" and is a sign that the dog is recovering from the virus. However, "blue eye"—edema or swelling of the cornea—can be a dangerous condition in its own right because it can cause blindness. It requires immediate veterinary attention.

Treatment. Because hepatitis is caused by a virus, no specific treatment is effective. But, as with distemper, antibiotics for secondary infection and good nursing care will usually help the dog to full recovery. The veterinarian may prescribe extra vitamins, a special diet with lots of fluids, and even blood transfusions. It's important to note that even when the dog is fully recovered, the hepatitis virus will be present in the urine for several months and may thus be transferred to healthy dogs.

Prevention. Temporary hepatitis immunity is transferred to the puppies from the mother, but only if she has been adequately vaccinated before the birth of the litter. Hepatitis vaccine is usually combined with the distemper vaccine and given at the same time—when the puppies are six to eight weeks old, and twice more until 16 weeks. Thereafter, the dog must get a booster shot every year.

It's appropriate here to talk about adenovirus type 2 and its use in protection against hepatitis. As mentioned earlier, infectious hepatitis is usually caused by adenovirus type 1. The type 2 virus, a very close relative of type 1, protects against type 1 infections (hepatitis itself) and against the common upper respiratory infection commonly caused by the type 2 virus. The real advantage of the type 2 vaccination is that it doesn't cause the eye problems that can result from the type 1 vaccine, and it's possible that in the future all infectious hepatitis vaccines will be type 2.

Leptospirosis

This is a serious bacterial disease that affects dogs, rats, cattle, and human beings. Because of the possibility of human infection, leptospirosis is regarded as a public health hazard. Two strains of leptospira bacteria can cause the disease in dogs. The bacteria primarily attack the kidneys. The disease is transmitted by direct contact with the urine of an infected animal.

Signs and diagnosis. A number of warning signs can indicate that the dog has leptospirosis. The most frequent signs are weakness, lack of appetite, high fever, vomiting, and diarrhea. The dog's urine may be a deep yellow color, and it may have mouth ulcers—red patches on the tongue and the edges of the gums. Accurate diagnosis is essential to successful treatment. In addition to noting the signs listed above, the veterinarian may run blood tests to help confirm the diagnosis.

Treatment. Once the diagnosis is made, leptospirosis can be treated with antibiotics such as penicillin and streptomycin. The dog will need careful nursing, and if it has become dehydrated, it may be necessary to rehydrate it with fluids administered intravenously. Vitamins are usually prescribed to help recovery.

Prevention. A puppy should be vaccinated against leptospirosis first at nine weeks old and again at 14 to 16 weeks. Thereafter, annual booster shots are necessary. If the dog is exposed to leptospirosis, the veterinarian may recommend a booster before the year is up. If there's an outbreak of leptospirosis in a kennel, all dogs must be boostered regardless of when they were last vaccinated. Another important preventive measure is rat control—rats carry the bacteria in their urine and the dog can easily be infected by contact with the rat urine.

Parvovirus

The virus group that parvovirus belongs to is not new to scientists, but until recently they didn't know it could affect dogs. So when the virus appeared in the U.S. in 1978, it caught both the scientists and public off guard. Nobody really knows where the canine parvovirus came from, though there is some indication that a mutation of the cat distemper virus (feline parvovirus) produced a new strain that affects dogs. The virus is spread in the stool, and it's been estimated that a single infected stool can carry over a billion particles of the virus. The disease is now found worldwide.

Signs and diagnosis. Dogs with parvovirus will usually vomit and have diarrhea; the diarrhea frequently is bloody and has an unpleasant odor. Most dogs develop a fever and have a low white blood cell count. The severity of the disease depends on the age of the dog. Puppies are the most susceptible and may become dehydrated and die in a very short time. Parvovirus can also cause heart muscle disease in very young puppies that are two to four weeks old. The veterinarian diagnoses parvovirus by running laboratory tests to detect the presence of antibodies in the blood; this is important because diarrhea and vomiting can also be signs of many other conditions. Although parvovirus is particularly dangerous to puppies, it's not unusual for older dogs to develop a mild infection that clears up with very little treatment.

Treatment. Unfortunately, parvovirus—like most viral conditions—does not respond to any specific treatment. Early diagnosis and intensive care are essential if a severely infected dog—especially a puppy—is to survive. Careful nursing is called for, and the dog will certainly need intravenous fluid therapy to counteract dehydration caused by the diarrhea. The infected premises must be cleaned with one part household bleach to 30 parts of water; this will kill the virus.

Prevention. This disease can be successfully prevented by vaccination. As with distemper and hepatitis, an adequately vaccinated female dog will provide temporary immunity to the pups; she should be vaccinated before she is bred. The puppies get a series of shots between the ages of nine weeks and 14 to 16 weeks; annual or semi-annual boosters are necessary for complete protection.

Coronavirus

Canine coronavirus is much less severe than parvoviral disease. The canine coronavirus invades and destroys the lining of the intestine.

Signs and diagnosis. Dogs with coronavirus will have similar signs to parvovirus but these signs will be less severe. Vomiting and diarrhea occur but recovery is often quick. Diagnosis is based on signs and symptoms. Electron microscopy and virus isolation are the only definitive methods of diagnosis.

Treatment. Coronavirus responds to symptomatic treatment. The principle objectives of treatment for coronavirus are to rest the GI tract, restore and maintain fluid and electrolyte balance, and minimize fluid losses. Food and water are withheld until vomiting has ceased for 24 hours and diarrhea is subsiding. Small amounts of water are introduced first and, if tolerated, feeding can begin. Frequent, small meals of a bland diet should be given for two to three days, with gradual reintroduction of the regular diet.

Prevention. Coronavirus can be prevented by vaccination. As with the other vaccinations discussed above, coronavirus vaccine needs to be started early and, after the last vaccination at four to six months, boostered annually. The enteric viruses are highly contagious and are principally transmitted by the fecal-oral route. The best method of control is cleanliness. Infected premises may be cleaned with one part household bleach to 30 parts of water; this will kill the virus.

Canine Respiratory Disease Complex

This disease is commonly known as "kennel cough" because of its primary symptom—a dry, deep cough—and its common occurrence in kennels or veterinary hospitals where a number of dogs are housed together. The disease can recur year after year, and although it's not usually serious, it causes a lot of grief to dog owners, kennel operators, and veterinarians.

It wasn't until fairly recently that scientists learned that kennel cough can be caused by a number of organisms—not just one. Among the viruses and bacteria that have been isolated as causes are adenovirus type 2, parainfluenza virus, canine herpes virus, and the *Bordetella bronchiseptica* bacterium. Because it usually affects the trachea—the windpipe—and the bronchial tubes, kennel cough is often referred to as "tracheobron-chitis."

Signs and diagnosis. In its mild form, kennel cough causes a dry, deep cough. Slight pressure on the windpipe can start the dog coughing spasmodically. A more severe form of the disease causes a deep, productive cough often accompanied by nasal and eye discharges. Pneumonia is a possible complication, and if the disease is not diagnosed and treated promptly, it can cause death in young dogs. Diagnosis is usually based on the clinical signs above, because isolating the exact causative organism is expensive and time-consuming.

Treatment. If bacteria are causing the condition, the dog can be successfully treated with antibiotics. If a virus is the culprit, no specific medications are effective. The veterinarian can, however, prescribe cough suppressants to quiet the dog and relieve its discomfort—owners appreciate this, too, because most infected dogs seem to cough more at night.

Prevention. At the moment, veterinarians can vaccinate against three of the many causes of kennel cough. A very effective parainfluenza virus vaccine is commonly given along with the combined shot for distemper, hepatitis, and leptospirosis. The adenovirus type 2 vaccine used to protect against hepatitis also protects against the respiratory disease caused by the type 2 virus. A vaccine is also available against *Bordetella bronchiseptica* bacteria. This can be given once or twice a year, depending on your vet's assessment of need.

These three protective measures can do a lot to cut down on the incidence of kennel cough. And in a kennel, additional protection can be provided by proper ventilation and the use of disinfectants that are effective in destroying viruses and bacteria. The veterinarian can recommend products for kennel use. If your dog is going to be in a high-exposure situation—around a lot of other dogs at a show or in a boarding kennel—ask your veterinarian's advice on a booster shot to give it extra protection against possible infection.

Rabies

Rabies is the canine disease everyone knows about. It's caused by a virus that affects the brain and, while all warm-blooded animals are susceptible, the animals most commonly affected in North America are dogs, cats, bats, foxes, raccoons, and skunks. The disease is transmitted by direct contact with the saliva of an infected animal. Because humans can be infected by contact with a rabid animal, and because there is no treatment for rabies, domestic animals must by law be vaccinated against the disease. Rabies laws are strictly enforced throughout the United States.

Signs and diagnosis. In dogs, rabies usually follows a two-stage pattern. The first stage is demonstrated by a change in behavior. For example, a very gentle dog may become noticeably more aggressive. This is followed by either paralysis or viciousness. In the paralytic form, the dog becomes unable to swallow and the lower jaw often drops open. In the vicious or "furious" form, the dog will attack anything in its way. Usually a rabid dog is dead within 10 days of the appearance of the first

UNDERSTANDING YOUR DOG'S VACCINATION RECORD

When you get your puppy's papers from the breeder, or check out the health record your veterinarian gives you when you take a dog for vaccinations, you'll see a whole bunch of abbreviations. What do they mean?

DM	These initials indicate a distemper-measles vaccine given to a very young puppy to impart immediate protection against distemper.
DMP	This is the distemper-measles vaccine plus parainfluenza, which is part of the canine respiratory disease complex commonly known as kennel cough.
DHL	This stands for distemper, hepatitis, and leptospirosis. It's also known as the "3 in 1" shot.
DA$_2$L	This is the same as the DHL except that the A2 indicates that the vaccine used was the adenovirus type 2 which, as explained in the discussion of hepatitis, protects against both hepatitis and respiratory disease caused by the type 2 virus.
DA$_2$LP-P	This is a frequently used combination and is essentially a "5 in 1" shot. The initials stand for distemper, adenovirus type 2 (against hepatitis), leptospirosis, parainfluenza, and—the final P—parvovirus.
DA$_2$LP-P-CV	This combination is the same as the "5 in 1" shot but has added coronavirus, thus CV.

As it becomes possible to vaccinate against more diseases, the abbreviations will certainly become longer and the "3 in 1"—which is already a "6 in 1"—may well become a "9 in 1."

symptoms. If a dog is suspected of having rabies, it must be destroyed and its brain checked for presence of the virus; this is the only way of confirming the diagnosis.

Treatment. If examination of the dog's brain reveals that the animal did have rabies, any person who had been bitten by the dog or exposed to its saliva must undergo rabies shots. The human diploid rabies vaccine now used in people who have been exposed to a rabid animal replaces the painful series of shots that used to be given. Early intervention is important. If the diploid vaccine is given before signs of rabies appear, the success rate is high. It's possible but rare for the vaccine, correctly used, to save the person once signs of the disease are present.

Prevention. By law, dogs must be vaccinated against rabies first at the age of four months and then either every year or every three years after that. The precise requirements depend on the law in your area, and your veterinarian will tell you what is required.

Note: If you ever suspect that your dog or any other animal has rabies, try to confine the animal without touching it—*never* touch an animal that you think may be rabid with your bare hands—and call the proper authorities. Usually it is only necessary to call the law enforcement agency for your district.

Zoonotic Diseases

The following is a list of diseases possibly transmitted from dog to human. Immunosuppressed individuals will be much more susceptible and should take precaution.

Streptococcal Infections

Streptococcal infections of dogs are caused primarily by group G streptococci. In households where strep throat is a chronic problem in humans, the supposition is that pets are reinfecting children. No clinical signs are evident in affected pets, and pets separated from infected people clear themselves of infection. Diagnosis is made with a dry swab culture of the tonsillar region.

Bite Infections

Dogs account for 80 to 90 percent of animal bites. The infecting organism in bite or scratch injuries usually corresponds to the normal oral microflora of dogs and cats. The type of injury following dog bite wounds varies, including abrasions, punctures, avulsions, and lacerations. Thorough washing of all bite wounds and scratches is essential.

Campylobacteriosis

Food animals serve as the primary reservoir for zoonotic campylobacteriosis. Pet animals are primarily inapparent carriers and usually shed the organisms only during the diarrheic episode. Clinical signs of campylobacteriosis in dogs usually include profuse watery diarrhea, which results in severe dehydration. People have severe diarrhea, fever, and acute abdominal pain.

Rabies

Rabies is probably the most serious zoonotic

disease. If a dog contracts rabies and bites a human, it is likely that the human will get rabies and die. Vaccination for dogs is mandatory in all areas of the United States and should be given annually or less often depending on the type of vaccine used.

Roundworms And Hookworms

Roundworms and hookworms are common intestinal parasites of dogs that are capable of infecting and inducing disease in humans who ingest the infective stages of the worms or have direct skin contact with hookworm larvae in the soil. Keeping pets free of worms and in good hygiene will prevent problems to humans.

PARASITES THAT BUG YOUR DOG

Parasites are a problem that most dog owners have to deal with at one time or another. Parasites are, by definition, organisms that survive by feeding off another creature, and the two types that may select your dog as their host are external parasites that live in or on the skin or in the ear canals, and internal parasites that inhabit the internal organs—usually the intestines.

External parasites all resemble insects, and some are so small that they cannot be seen with the naked eye. The external parasites most commonly found on dogs are fleas, ticks, lice, mange mites, and ear mites. Most of them are highly contagious, and if one dog in a household is infected, other dogs in the same household are likely to be infected, too. These parasites cause severe itching, skin infections, and loss of hair. You can control external parasites with insecticides that you use both on the animal and on the environment—many of these pests live part of their life off the dog in the grass of your lawn or in convenient nooks and crannies in your home. The medication you use will depend on the type of parasite you're dealing with, and your veterinarian can identify the problem and suggest a suitable insecticide.

The most common internal parasites live in the dog's intestines, and if they're left untreated, they can cause serious problems like chronic diarrhea,

anemia, poor condition of coat, and cough. Some
internal parasites attack other organs, like the
heart. All dogs are susceptible to internal parasites.

Unlike some external parasites, which you may
(after some experience of dog ownership) be able
to identify and treat yourself with a topical product such as a flea powder, internal parasites always
require professional veterinary attention. Although
you should be able to recognize the signs of a
possible problem, you should never try to diagnose
or treat internal parasites yourself. Your veterinarian will make the diagnosis by examining a sample
of the dog's feces under a microscope. In most
cases, the vet is looking not for the parasite itself
but for the minute eggs that the organism deposits
in the stool. Once the diagnosis is made, the veterinarian will prescribe the appropriate medication.
Don't ever medicate for internal parasites without
professional advice—worming medicines are poisons and should not be administered at random.

The internal parasites that most commonly
infect the dog's intestines are roundworms, hookworms, whipworms, tapeworms, giardia, and coccidia. The potentially very dangerous heartworm
affects the dog's heart.

The following discussion of parasites will help
you recognize the signs of parasitic infestation.

External Parasites

Fleas

Fleas are tiny brown insects that live on the dog's
skin and feed by sucking the animal's blood. If you

part the dog's fur, you can see them moving. Fleas can't fly, but they can jump quite a distance and travel easily from one dog to another. They irritate the skin and make the dog scratch—although not all scratching dogs have fleas. And the saliva of the flea is a potent allergen that can set up a severe allergic reaction in a susceptible dog. In such a case, the dog will lose a great deal of hair, especially above the tail, and develop scaly skin on its back. It will probably scratch itself so persistently that the skin bleeds. This is known as flea-bite dermatitis.

Besides irritating the skin, the flea is the intermediate host of the tapeworm—an internal parasite which is described later in this chapter.

In some parts of the United States, fleas are a year-round problem. In the northern climates, the winter cold will kill fleas outdoors; they can, however, winter comfortably in your home.

Life cycle. The adult flea lays its eggs on the dog or in the environment—on the lawn, in the dog's bed, in your carpet. The eggs laid on the dog fall off and, after a period that varies from one to 10 days depending on environmental temperature and humidity, hatch into legless larvae—the immature form of the insect. After feeding for five to 11 days on the ground, the larvae spin cocoons in which they remain for five days to five weeks. Again, the length of time depends on environmental conditions. The adult fleas emerge from the cocoons and hop onto the dog. The female fleas reproduce almost immediately, and the cycle starts again.

Signs and diagnosis. The most common indication that a dog has fleas is extreme itching. But don't assume that the itching is caused by fleas unless you actually see them. Spread the dog's fur on the rump or in the groin and look for the adult fleas running through the fur. Another way to check is to rub the animal's rump vigorously onto a wet, white paper towel. Flea feces are mostly blood, and any black specks that fall on the towel and smear to a reddish-brown color are evidence of flea infestation. As mentioned earlier, an allergic reaction to prolonged exposure to the fleas' saliva may cause hair loss, scaliness on the back, and raw patches where the dog has scratched itself. It is preferable for you to get rid of the fleas before this happens.

Control and treatment. Control of fleas can be a wearisome business, and you'll need the advice of your veterinarian and, possibly, an exterminator. You must treat the affected dog and all the other animals in the household, and you must also treat the animals' indoor and, in some cases, outdoor environment.

Insect growth regulators (IGRs) should be used to stop the life cycle of the flea. These chemicals were developed to interfere with the second stage larva and prevent it from further developing into the adult. Further research indicates that IGRs may also prevent the egg from hatching by affecting the adult female. The IGRs have revolutionized the flea-fighting industry. Using IGRs with adulticides in the environment and ridding the dog of adult fleas are sure ways to stop the pest.

A number of dog shampoos and dips are available that will effectively kill the fleas. Sprays and powders are quick and effective. Ask your veterinarian to recommend a product, and use it strictly according to the manufacturer's instructions. Remember that any insecticide you use on your pet can cause side effects like vomiting, excess salivation, or skin irritation. Check before you use the product that you know what to do if there are side effects. A flea collar can help keep the animal from becoming reinfested. If the dog has scratched itself raw, cortisone given orally or by injection should clear up the condition.

Once you've treated the animal or animals, thoroughly clean the house, the dog's kennel, and any other areas where the fleas may breed. Your veterinarian can recommend an insecticide, frequently a spray that will fog the infested area.

Ticks

Ticks are small, insect-like creatures that usually inhabit the parts of the dog where the hair is thin. They bury their heads in the skin and suck the animal's blood. Although they can be found anywhere on the body, they seem to prefer the head area, especially around the ears. When they are swollen with blood, ticks are about the size of a pea. Usually, the only result of a tick bite is mild irritation. Ticks can carry a number of diseases such as Lyme disease, Ehrlichia canis, Babesiosis, and tick paralysis—to name a few.

Life cycle. After gorging itself on the dog's blood, the female tick drops off and lays its eggs in a crack or crevice indoors or outdoors, where they incubate and then hatch into larvae or "seed ticks."

These attach themselves to the dog and feed on the blood, then fall to the ground and, after a week or two, molt to their next stage of development—the nymph stage. Again, they find the dog, feed, fall off, and molt to the adult stage. The adult male and female ticks mate, and the cycle repeats. If the whole cycle occurs in your home, your dog will be continuously infected. If the cycle occurs outside, your dog or any other dog that enters the area can become infected. Your dog will also bring the ticks into the house.

Signs and diagnosis. The signs of tick infection aren't always as obvious as you might expect. The dog won't usually scratch excessively, and unless you actually see and remove them, the ticks can live a long life. The best way of keeping your animal clear of this parasite is to check the skin regularly around the head, ears, and neck, under the arms, and in any other thin-haired area.

If the tick is of the type that carries a neurotoxin, tick paralysis will develop. The neurotoxin in the tick's saliva enters the dog's bloodstream and signs of paralysis appear within 36 hours. The dog becomes progressively weaker, and the paralysis spreads to the back legs, the front legs, and then to the respiratory system.

Control and treatment. As with fleas, getting rid of ticks involves treating both the dog and its surroundings. If there are only a few ticks on the animal, remove them with tweezers. Use the tweezers to grasp the tick where its head is embedded in the skin, and pull the tick out. Destroy the tick after removal. Try to remove the whole tick; if the head is left embedded in the dog's skin, it may cause a sore. Don't ever use a cigarette to remove a tick from the dog's skin.

If your dog is heavily infected, bathe it with an insecticidal solution recommended by your veterinarian. Put a tick collar on the dog and use sprays or powders periodically, as directed by the vet, to help keep the dog free of further tick problems.

When you've treated the dog, treat the environment. You can use an insecticide to fog your home. Sprays are also available to use in your yard or on other areas where the ticks may be hiding. Ask your veterinarian where you should apply insecticide. In the case of a severe infestation, you may also need to get the advice of an exterminator.

In the case of tick paralysis, prompt treatment should lead to complete recovery within a matter of hours. Remove the ticks and take the dog immediately to the veterinarian, who will bathe the dog with an insecticide solution to destroy any ticks you have not already removed. As soon as the toxin ceases to enter the bloodstream, recovery begins. Untreated, however, tick paralysis is fatal. Ehrlichia canis and Babesiosis are diseases that cause anemia, while Lyme disease causes fever and lameness.

Lice

Lice are tiny wingless insects, barely visible to the naked eye, that live their entire life cycle on the dog. There are a number of different types of lice, but each type is host-specific—that is, it can only live on one species of animal. Dog lice live only on dogs and can't survive on cats or humans;

human lice don't infect animals. The lice pass from one host to another by direct contact, and can be found on all parts of the body.

Life cycle. The female lice lay eggs on the dog but, unlike the flea eggs which fall off the animal, these eggs (or nits) are attached to the hair shaft. They are small, white particles and look a bit like human dandruff. The parasite lives out its life and reproductive cycle on the dog.

Signs and diagnosis. The signs of infection are usually limited to itching. If the infestation is severe, the dog may scratch itself raw.

Control and treatment. It's important to have lice identified by your veterinarian, but once you know what you're dealing with, treatment is straightforward and successful. Lice are easier to get rid of than some of the other external parasites. Because they live out their full cycle on the dog, it's only necessary to treat the animal. If there's more than one dog in the family, however, it is necessary to treat them all since they will certainly have passed the lice to one another.

Your veterinarian can recommend a dog shampoo, dip, or spray to get rid of the lice. You'll probably have to repeat the treatment at weekly intervals for three weeks. Read the label on the product carefully and follow instructions. If the dog has scratched itself raw, the veterinarian will prescribe medication to heal the lesions.

Mange Mites

Mites are small, insect-like parasites that spend their whole life cycle on the dog and will live only a short time off the animal. They are very small and can't be seen without a microscope. Like lice, mange mites are host-specific. Most animal species are susceptible to some type of mange mite, but the types that affect dogs won't affect cats or people, and vice versa. Of the several types of mange mites that affect dogs, the most common are sarcoptic and demodectic mites.

Sarcoptic Mange

Sarcoptic mange, commonly known as "scabies," is caused by a microscopic, round, four-legged mite. It's highly contagious between dogs.

Life cycle. The female mite tunnels into the skin and lays eggs which hatch in 10 to 14 days. The dog hosts the mites for their entire life cycle.

Signs and diagnosis. The signs of sarcoptic mange vary, but the most common are scaliness and loss of hair around the edges of the ears and on the elbows, chest, and back. Intense itching is a characteristic of this condition. Your veterinarian diagnoses sarcoptic mange by scraping a suspected lesion and examining it under a microscope for the presence of the mite or its eggs. Skin scrapings, however, do not always reveal the presence of the culprit and here it's possible that you may be able to help. If you have developed small marks similar to mosquito bites on your own body, the mange mite may be responsible. Although the mite cannot live on humans, it will bite.

Control and treatment. Your veterinarian will prescribe an insecticide to cure sarcoptic mange. You'll probably need to apply the medication weekly for three weeks to get rid of the mites completely, and all dogs in the household must be treated at the same time. Lime-sulphur dips and other miticides give good results. Recently, the use of the drug Ivermectin by injection has proven curative in most cases. Long-haired dogs that are severely infected should be clipped before treatment. Your vet can also prescribe medications to control itching and prevent further skin infection.

Demodectic Mange

This type of mange is often called "red mange" and is caused by a microscopic mite that has an elongated shape and lives deep in the skin in hair follicles. Demodectic mange can be localized to one or two areas of the dog's body or generalized over the whole body. A curious property of this parasite is that you may never know the dog has got it because the animal's defense mechanisms keep it under control. Perhaps 50 or 60 percent of all dogs have the infection but show no signs of it, and a perfectly normal female dog who has never shown any signs of demodectic mange can be a carrier and infect all her pups.

Life cycle. The only way demodectic mange mites can be transferred is from the mother to the puppy at birth. The mites live dormant in the skin until the puppy is about four months old, at which point they become active and the puppy usually begins to show signs of hair loss, particularly around the muzzle, eyes, and forelimbs.

Signs and diagnosis. As mentioned above, hair loss is the first indicator of demodectic mange. In severe cases, secondary bacterial infections can cause the skin to become thickened and inflamed. Sometimes, but not always, the dog will scratch to relieve itching caused by the condition. Your veterinarian can diagnose the demodectic mange only from microscopic examination of skin scrapings from a suspected area.

Control and treatment. Many insecticidal preparations have been put forward as cures for demodectic mange, but in fact treatment has until recently proven very disappointing. Localized lesions often respond well to treatment, but generalized demodectic mange has always been very frustrating to the owner and the veterinarian. Since recovery often depends on the body's own defense mechanism, the dog must be in top shape for the defense mechanism (antibodies) to work properly. This means that the dog must be well fed, free of any other parasites, and not under undue stress. Antibiotics are used to control secondary infection. The drug Amitraz has become available and has proven very effective in eliminating the demodectic mange mite. Amitraz is available only through your veterinarian and has proven 99 percent effective in curing this once dreaded parasitic disease.

Ear Mites

Ear mites, often called "ear mange," are insect-like creatures that resemble the sarcoptic mange mite. They live in the ear canal—hence the name—and can barely be seen with the naked eye.

Life cycle. The ear mite lives its whole life in the ear canal. Occasionally a few travel to other parts of the body, but these wanderers don't seem to cause any problems. The mite is host-specific and is highly contagious between animals of the same species.

Signs and diagnosis. Several clues can warn you that your dog has ear mites. Head-shaking and intense itching are often the first signs (but these signs can also indicate ear problems other than mites). Often there's a brown, waxy material in the ears, and if a secondary infection has set in, the ear canal will emit an unpleasant odor.

Control and treatment. Ear mites respond well to treatment, and in many cases you won't even need to see the veterinarian. Thorough daily cleaning of the ears with cotton swabs is a must (the grooming section tells you how to do it), and often plain mineral oil dropped in the ears after every cleaning is enough to kill the mites. This daily cleaning should be continued for 10 to 14 days. However, if the dog is still obviously distressed after a few days, see a veterinarian. If home treatment doesn't work, your veterinarian will prescribe medication. If one dog in the household has ear mites, you must treat all the animals in the house at the same time, even if their ears don't seem to be infected, and repeat the treatment daily for 10 to 14 days to make sure that all of the mites are dead.

If the smell of the ears indicates that a secondary infection has set in, your veterinarian will prescribe an antibiotic ointment. Remember that if home treatment does not seem to work within three to four days, you should consult the veterinarian.

Internal Parasites

Roundworms

These are long, white worms that look like spaghetti, and they're easy to recognize in the dog's stool or vomit. It's probably safe to assume that most puppies will contract roundworms from their mother, but older dogs usually become resistant to them. Under normal sanitary conditions, these parasites are not such a serious problem as other, faster-developing parasites.

Life cycle. The most common method of infection is through the uterus of the mother dog. Scientists have learned that the dormant, microscopic larvae present in the mother become active when she's about 42 days pregnant. The larvae (immature roundworms) migrate from the mother's tissues to those of the puppies while they are still in the uterus. After the pup is born, the larvae either develop into adult worms in the pup's intestine, or remain dormant in the tissues and become active when the puppy is older. In the case of a female, these dormant larvae will become active during her pregnancy and, in turn, infect her puppies. Another method of infection is through the mother's milk. The larvae pass to the puppy through the milk and develop in the same way as those passed before birth.

Roundworm infections aren't limited to puppies. Older dogs can develop roundworms from contact with stools passed by an infected dog. However, older dogs usually become resistant to roundworms and commonly pass them out either in the stool or in vomit.

Signs and diagnosis. Puppies heavily infected with roundworms are thin and usually have diarrhea. Sometimes they look pot-bellied, but this by itself isn't sufficient proof of infection. Often you'll know for sure because the puppy passes the spaghetti-like worms in the stool, or vomits them up. Your veterinarian makes the diagnosis by analyzing the stool.

Control and treatment. The best method of control is to have stool samples checked periodically. If there's a problem, remove the infected stool immediately after the dog defecates in order to avoid reinfection, and worm the dog according to your veterinarian's recommendation. Contrary to what some people think, it's *not* necessary to worm a dog monthly to control roundworms. Over-medication can cause serious problems like vomiting and diarrhea, so medicate only on the advice of your veterinarian.

Hookworms

Hookworms are small parasites (less than half an inch long) that affect dogs of all ages, although young puppies seem to be more severely affected than older dogs. The parasites live in the small intestine and attach themselves to the lining of the intestine. Hookworms are blood-suckers, and if there are enough of them they can cause severe anemia and even death.

Life cycle. Under ideal hot and humid conditions, hookworm eggs passed in the stool of an infected dog incubate very quickly—within 24 hours—to the immature larva stage, at which they become active and can infect any dog that comes in contact with them. All the dog has to do to become infected is walk on the soil where the eggs or larvae are present. The larvae can penetrate the skin directly, or the eggs can enter the dog's system when it licks them off its feet and swallows them.

Signs and diagnosis. As mentioned earlier, young puppies are particularly affected by hookworms. Young animals that are infected look very thin, and their fur is scruffy and dull. Diarrhea tinged with blood is common in both young and older dogs. The veterinarian diagnoses hookworms by microscopic examination of the stool.

Control and treatment. Hookworm infestation is treated with medications specifically indicated for this parasite. Your veterinarian will set up a worming routine for your dog, and just as important as the medication is environmental clean-up. Your dog will become reinfected time and again if the ground where it walks remains infected. And remember that it can reinfect itself from its own stools, so they must be removed promptly. You can get yard sprays to kill the hookworm eggs, but continuing attention to sanitation is of the utmost importance. Having your veterinarian check stool samples regularly is the most practical method of controlling hookworms.

Whipworms

Whipworms affect dogs of all ages and live in the dog's cecum—the short, closed end sac of the lower intestinal tract. The whipworm is very small and can rarely be seen with the naked eye, and it gets the name from the shape of its body: The top half is long and thin and the back part is short and thick.

Life cycle. A dog becomes infested with whipworms by walking on contaminated ground soil and then licking the eggs from its feet. The whipworm eggs are thickwalled and very hard to destroy, so they can stay in the soil for long periods. In northern climates they winter and become a severe problem when the soil begins to thaw in the spring. The ingested eggs develop into adult worms in the dog's intestine, lay eggs which are passed in the stool, and so continue the cycle.

Signs and diagnosis. The most significant effect of whipworm infection is inflammation of the bowel which causes intermittent bouts of diarrhea. If your dog has been having diarrhea off and on and you've ruled out other possible causes, it's possible that it's got whipworms.

Control and treatment. Your veterinarian will diagnose whipworms from a microscopic examination of the stool, and he or she can choose from a number of remedies for treating them. However, because poor sanitation is a frequent cause of whipworm infestation, environmental control is as important as medication. Reinfestation is a frequent problem and you may find that you have to worm your dog, on your veterinarian's recommendation, several times a year. Try to forestall problems by having your veterinarian check stool samples regularly (frequency depends on the climate in your

area), keeping your yard clean, and keeping your
dog away from areas where you know owners don't
clean up after their dogs.

Tapeworms

Tapeworms are flat and, traditionally, got their
name from their shape and their resemblance to
pieces of tape. In fact, tapeworm segments passed
in the dog's stool look like grains of rice. It's possible to see them moving as they are passed. Each
segment is an egg packet containing a large number
of eggs.

Life cycle. Unlike roundworms, hookworms, and
whipworms, tapeworms are not transmitted directly from the stool. Tapeworm infection occurs
when the dog eats an infected intermediate host—
in this country the flea is most likely to be the
culprit. The flea has already fed on the tapeworm
eggs contained in the segments passed in the stool
of an infected animal. Inside the flea, the eggs
mature to the stage at which they can infect a dog.
The flea lives in the dog's fur and, in the process of
grooming itself, the dog swallows the flea. As the
flea is digested the eggs are released in the dog's
intestine and grow to adult size. These adult tapeworms, in turn, lay eggs contained in segments
which are passed in the dog's stool, and the cycle
starts over. Mice, rabbits, and fish can also act as
intermediate hosts for the tapeworm. So can cattle
and pigs, and a dog that eats raw meat from any of
these hosts can become infected.

Signs and diagnosis. Tapeworms seldom cause
much real trouble beyond mild diarrhea and some

rectal itching. You're most likely to spot them by examining the hair around the rectum for the rice-like segments that contain the tapeworm eggs.

Control and treatment. As with so many parasite problems, treating tapeworms is a two-part task—you have to rid the dog of tapeworms and rid the environment of the intermediate host. Your veterinarian can treat the dog for tapeworms with an oral or injected medication. If the dog is getting the tapeworms from fleas, however, you won't make any progress unless you get rid of the fleas, too. The section on external parasites tells you how.

Coccidia

Unlike the intestinal parasites discussed so far, this parasite is not a worm. It's a one-celled organism (protozoan) that lives in the intestine and usually causes problems in very young puppies. You can only see it under a microscope.

Life cycle. Coccidia multiply rapidly in the lining of the intestines and are transferred from one animal to another in the stool.

Signs and diagnosis. Very young puppies are usually most susceptible to coccidia, and this parasite is often found in puppies that have been housed with a lot of companions in unsanitary conditions. Typical warning signs are emaciated appearance and diarrhea which sometimes contains blood. Very often, secondary infections cause discharge from the eyes or nose.

Control and treatment. If it's not severe, coccidia infection is self-limiting and disappears when the surroundings are returned to a sanitary condition.

However, medications are available, and your veterinarian can prescribe medication for the dog and make suggestions for maintaining a clean environment.

Giardia

Giardia parasites are similar to coccidia in that they are also one-celled organisms. Giardia, however, can move around by means of a hair-like structure called the flagellum.

Life cycle. This parasite lives in the intestines and is transferred in the stool. Its life cycle is perpetuated by unsanitary conditions. It seems to be triggered to activity by stress, and the "cyst" or nonactive form of giardia can be carried by dogs with no apparent ill effects. When the dog's under stress, however—for instance, when the animal gets ill or moves to a strange environment—the parasites become active and the dog begins to show signs of infection.

Signs and diagnosis. Puppies that are housed with other puppies in unsanitary conditions are very susceptible to this parasite—in fact, it's a grossly overlooked disease among puppies. The most common sign of trouble is diarrhea that contains blood or mucus. Any puppy that has diarrhea that won't clear up with conventional treatment may be infested with giardia.

The veterinarian diagnoses giardia from a stool sample, but the method of examination is different from that used for other internal parasites. In this case, the veterinarian does a direct fecal smear, which involves taking a very fresh stool sample—

not more than 15 to 20 minutes old—and examining a drop of it for the moving parasite.

Control and treatment. Medications can clear up giardia very quickly, but as with other parasites it's equally important to improve the cleanliness of the environment.

Heartworm

Heartworm disease is caused by a nematode (worm) that lives in its adult stage in the right side of the dog's heart. Heartworms are transmitted from one dog to another by mosquitoes and do their damage in the adult stage, by which time the worms can be up to 12 inches long. Because the infection is transmitted by mosquitoes, heartworm disease used to be a real problem only in the warm, southern coastal areas of the United States. Increased mobility of the population (and its dogs) has caused the disease to spread widely, and it is becoming a very serious threat to dogs in most areas of the country.

Life cycle. There are three stages in the life cycle of the heartworm: 1) The adult female worm lays live immature worms in the infected dog's bloodstream. 2) These immature worms can only develop further in the mosquito, so they remain in the dog's bloodstream until the animal is bitten by a mosquito. They then develop inside the mosquito to the infective larva stage; this process takes about two weeks. 3) The infected mosquito bites an uninfected dog and passes the infective larvae into the dog's bloodstream. The larvae live in the dog for about three months and then migrate to the dog's heart and settle in the right ventricle of the heart and the adjoining blood vessels. Within another three months, the worms are fully grown; they begin to reproduce, and the cycle starts over.

Signs and diagnosis. Severe infection of adult heartworms causes cough, breathing difficulties, fatigue, and general weakness. As the disease progresses, the dog's heart, liver, and lungs become severely damaged. Visible symptoms of the disease do not appear until the advanced stages, so it's important to have the dog checked regularly in order to arrest the disease in the early stages.

Control and treatment. Prevention of heartworm disease is better than cure—in fact, if the disease has reached an advanced stage before it is diagnosed, cure may be impossible. Your dog should be checked regularly for heartworms at intervals that your veterinarian will recommend according to where you live. Preventive medication is available and should be given daily or monthly throughout the mosquito season.

If the blood test administered by the veterinarian reveals the presence of heartworms, medications are prescribed. It may require several treatments with different medications to clear the dog of both the adult and immature worms. Once this treatment is completed, the dog should be given daily or monthly medication to prevent further infection. This preventive medication, however, can be given only to dogs that are free of established heartworm infection; in an infected dog, it can cause a severe or fatal reaction.

Dealing With An Emergency

Have you ever seen a dog injured in a fight or hit by a car? Perhaps you could only shake your head and walk away. Not because you didn't care, but because you didn't know how to approach and examine the dog, or what to do next. Especially if you have a dog of your own, you'll want to be prepared, for your dog depends on you for help in an emergency situation.

The First Aid section of this book lists the most common emergencies alphabetically. When the nature of an injury or condition is not readily apparent, signs are listed at the beginning of the section to help you identify the problem.

The purpose of first aid is to relieve suffering and stabilize your dog's vital signs until professional help is obtained. This book will give you the information and techniques you'll need to confidently administer first aid, and perhaps save the life of a pet. Clear directions are listed step-by-step. These directions are further clarified with dozens of illustrations.

The "why" of these procedures is explained in the back of the book. This section also includes preventive measures that can eliminate or minimize some hazards that could be dangerous to your pet.

Because minutes count in an emergency situation, you'll want to have a first aid kit prepared. It needn't be elaborate; suggested items are listed on page 220. Keep the kit and this book together in a convenient place, and take both with you when you travel with your dog.

We suggest you take the time to thoroughly familiarize yourself with the First Aid procedures. Certain sections are especially important. When a dog is choking or unconscious, speed is vital if the dog is to live. Therefore, it is of primary importance that you know how to give artificial respiration and CPR (cardiopulmonary resuscitation). It will also be most helpful if you know exactly how to approach and restrain a dog if an accident does occur. Again, minutes count.

In addition to the information you'll need to contact your own veterinarian, there is a line below to list the phone number of the Poison Control Center in your area. You will find them very helpful should it become necessary to contact them. The information operator can supply the number.

EMERGENCY INFORMATION

VETERINARIAN'S
NAME:_____

EMERGENCY
PHONE:_____

HOSPITAL
PHONE:_____

HOSPITAL
ADDRESS:_____

POISON CONTROL
CENTER PHONE:_____

Restraining An Injured Dog

STEP 1: Approach slowly, speaking in a reassuring tone of voice.

STEP 2: Move close to the dog without touching it.

STEP 3: Stoop down to the dog. While continuing to speak, observe its eyes and facial expression.

a. If the dog is wide-eyed and growling, DO NOT attempt to pet it. Proceed to Step 4.

b. If the dog is shivering, with its head lowered and a "smiling" appearance to its mouth, pet the dog for reassurance, first under the jaw. If this is permitted, pet the dog on the head.

Step 3b

continued

STEP 4: Slip a leash around the dog's neck. Use whatever material is available—rope, tie, belt, or torn rags.

STEP 5: If you are alone, place the leash around a fixed object, such as a fence post. Pull the dog against this object and tie the leash so the dog cannot move its head.

STEP 6: Muzzle the dog to protect yourself. If the dog is very short-muzzled, proceed to Step 7.

a. Using a long piece of rope, torn rags, or a tie, loop over the dog's muzzle and tie a single knot under the chin.

b. Bring the ends behind the ears and tie them in a bow.

Step 6a

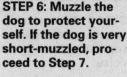

Step 6b

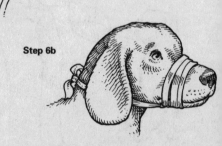

Step 7a

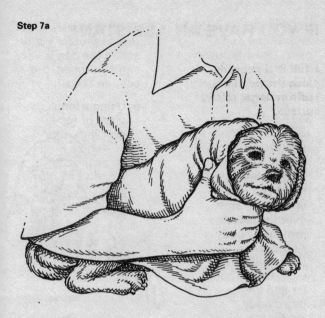

**STEP 7: If the dog is
very short-muzzled,
restrain it with a
towel.**

a. Wrap the towel
   around the dog's
   neck and hold
   the towel in
   front of its head.

b. If you are alone,
   pin the towel in
   place.

**STEP 8: If you are
alone, proceed to
administer treat-
ment.**

continued

IF YOU HAVE AN ASSISTANT

STEP 9: If possible, place the dog on a table or other raised surface.

a. If the dog is small, grasp its collar with one hand and place your other arm over its back and around its body. At the same time, pull forward on the collar and lift the dog's body, cradling it against your body.

Step 9a

Step 9b

b. If the dog is large, slip one arm under its neck, holding its throat in the crook of your arm. Be sure the dog can breathe easily. Place your other arm under the dog's stomach. Lift with both arms.

118

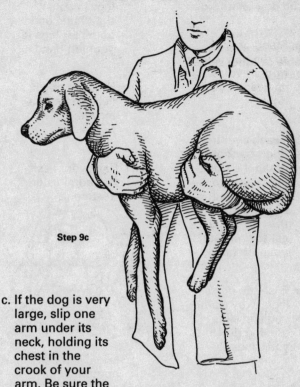

Step 9c

c. If the dog is very large, slip one arm under its neck, holding its chest in the crook of your arm. Be sure the dog can breathe easily. Place your other arm under the dog's rump and, pressing your arms toward one another, lift the dog.

d. Have your assistant administer treatment while you hold the dog on the table.

continued

119

STEP 10: If you want the dog on its side:

a. Stand or kneel so the dog is in front of you with its head to your right.

b. Reach over the dog's back and grasp the front leg closest to you with your right hand, and the rear leg closest to you with your left hand.

c. Push the dog's legs away from you and slide the dog down your body.

d. Grasp both front legs in your right hand and both rear legs in your left hand.

e. Hold the dog's neck down gently with your right arm.

f. Have your assistant administer treatment.

Step 10b

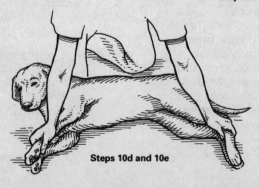

Steps 10d and 10e

120

STEP 11: If you want the dog sitting:

a. Slip one arm under the dog's neck, holding its throat in the crook of your arm. Be sure the dog can breathe easily.

Steps 11a and 11b

b. Place your other arm over the dog's back and around its stomach.

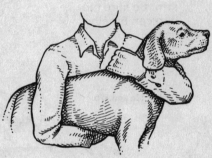

Step 11c

c. Pressing the dog against your body, apply body weight to the dog's rear quarters.

continued

121

d. Have your assistant administer treatment.

STEP 12: If you want the dog standing:

a. Slip one arm under the dog's neck, holding its throat in the crook of your arm. Be sure the dog can breathe easily.

b. Place your other arm under the dog's stomach.

c. Press the dog toward your body and lift upward.

d. Have your assistant administer treatment.

Steps 12a and 12b

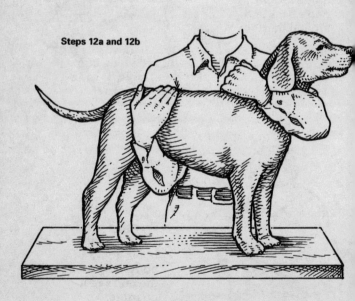

Transporting An Injured Dog

A. IF THE DOG NEEDS A STRETCHER

> *A flat board must be used if a broken back is suspected.*

STEP 1: Use a blanket or flat board as a stretcher. If you are using a board, proceed to Step 2. If you are using a blanket:

a. Place one hand under the dog's chest and the other under its rear; carefully lift or slide the dog onto the blanket.

b. Transport to the veterinarian.

STEP 2: If you are using a flat board:

a. Depending on the size of the dog, use a table leaf, ironing board, TV table top, large cutting board, or removable bookshelf. Make sure whatever you use will fit in your car.

b. Place two or three long strips of cloth or rope equidistant under the board, avoiding the area where the dog's neck will rest.

Step 1a

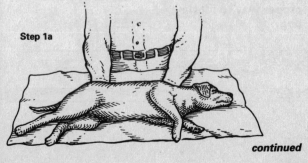

continued

c. Place one hand under the dog's chest and the other under its rear; carefully lift or slide the dog onto the board.

d. Tie the dog to the board.

e. Transport to the veterinarian.

Step 2d

B. IF THE DOG CAN BE LIFTED

STEP 1: Refer to pages 118-119 for the proper way to lift the dog.

STEP 2: Transport to the veterinarian.

Administering Oral Medicine

A. LIQUIDS

STEP 1: If you have an assistant, restrain the dog. See page 115.

a. Relieve the dog's apprehension by talking quietly and reassuringly.

b. Slip one arm under the dog's neck, holding its throat gently in the crook of your arm. Be sure the dog can breathe easily.

c. Pass the other arm over or under the middle of the dog, using gentle but firm pressure to hold its body against yours.

d. If necessary, apply a mouth-tie loosely so there is only slight jaw movement. See page 116.

> *If the dog is hard to handle, you will need help restraining it.*

Steps 1b and 1c

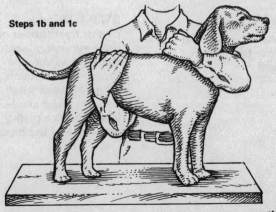

continued

STEP 2: Gently tip the dog's head slightly backwards.

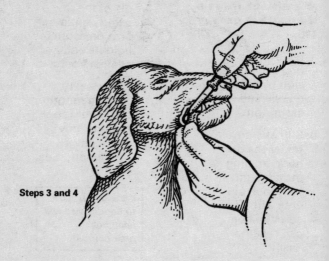

Steps 3 and 4

STEP 3: Pull the lower lip out at the corner to make a pouch.

STEP 4: Using a plastic eyedropper or dose syringe, place the fluid a little at a time into the pouch, allowing each small amount to be swallowed before giving any more of the dose.

STEP 5: Gently rub the throat to stimulate swallowing.

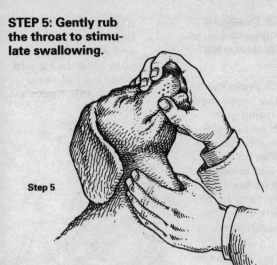

Step 5

B. PILLS

STEP 1: If you have an assistant, restrain the dog. See page 115.

a. Relieve the dog's apprehension by talking quietly and reassuringly.

b. Slip one arm under the dog's neck, holding its throat gently in the crook of your arm. Be sure the dog can breathe easily.

c. Pass the other arm over or under the middle of the dog, using gentle but firm pressure to hold its body against yours.

continued

STEP 2: Grasp the dog's upper jaw with one hand over its muzzle.

STEP 3: Press the lips over the upper teeth by pressing your thumb on one side and your fingers on the other so the dog's lips are between its teeth and your fingers. Firm pressure will force the mouth open.

STEP 4: Hold the pill between the thumb and index finger of your other hand, and place the pill as far back in the mouth as possible.

Steps 2, 3, and 4

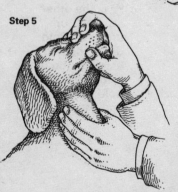

Step 5

STEP 5: Gently rub the dog's throat to help stimulate swallowing.

Animal Bite

STEP 1: Restrain the dog if necessary. See page 115.

STEP 2: Clip the hair around the wound.

STEP 3: Flush thoroughly by pouring 3% hydrogen peroxide into the wound. DO NOT use any other antiseptic.

STEP 4: Examine the wound. If the tissue under the wound appears to pass by when you move the skin, the wound will probably require stitches.

STEP 5: DO NOT bandage. Allow the wound to drain unless there is excessive bleeding. If the wound does bleed excessively, follow these steps:

a. Cover wound with a clean cloth, a sterile dressing, or sanitary napkin.

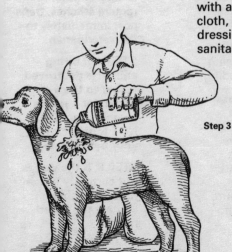

Step 3

continued

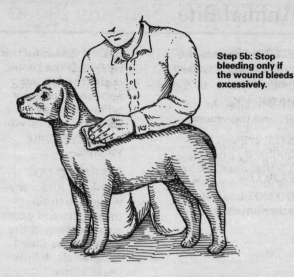

Step 5b: Stop bleeding only if the wound bleeds excessively.

b. Place your hand over the dressing and press firmly.

c. Keep pressure on the dressing to stop bleeding.

d. If blood soaks through the dressing, DO NOT remove. Apply more dressing and continue to apply pressure until bleeding stops.

STEP 6: If the wound is deep enough to require stitches, transport immediately to the veterinarian.

STEP 7: If biting animal is destroyed, take it to the veterinarian for a rabies examination. DO NOT touch it with your bare hands.

STEP 8: If the dog is not currently vaccinated for rabies, contact the veterinarian.

BLEEDING: Spurting Blood

WATCH FOR SIGNS OF SHOCK: PALE OR WHITE GUMS, RAPID HEARTBEAT AND BREATHING. IF SIGNS ARE PRESENT, SEE PAGE 192.

A. ON HEAD OR TORSO

STEP 1: Restrain the dog if necessary. See page 115.

STEP 2: Cover the wound with a sterile gauze pad, clean folded towel, or sanitary napkin.

STEP 3: Wrap torn rags or other soft material around the dressing and tie or tape just tightly enough to hold in place.

STEP 4: Transport immediately to the veterinarian.

> *If any wound is spurting blood, it means an artery has been cut. This requires immediate professional attention.*

Step 2

continued

B. ON LEGS OR TAIL

STEP 1: Restrain the dog if necessary. See page 115.

STEP 2: Apply a tourniquet.

a. Use a tie, belt, or piece of cloth folded to about one inch width. DO NOT use rope, wire, or string.

b. Place the material between the wound and the heart an inch or two above, but not touching, the wound.

Steps 2b and 2c

c. Wrap the tie or cloth twice around the appendage and cross the ends.

d. Tie a stick or ruler to the material with a single knot.

Step 2d

e. Twist the stick
   until bleeding
   stops, but no
   tighter.

Step 2e

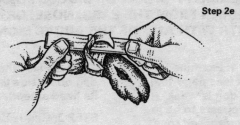

f. Wrap a piece of
   cloth around the
   stick and limb to
   keep in place.

Step 2f

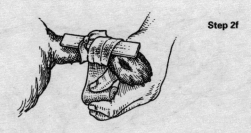

**STEP 3: If it will take
time to reach the
veterinarian, loosen
the tourniquet every
15 minutes for a
period of 1-2 minutes
and then tighten
again.**

**STEP 4: Transport
immediately to the
veterinarian.**

133

BLEEDING: Internal

SIGNS: PALE OR WHITE GUMS; RAPID HEARTBEAT AND BREATHING; AVAILABILITY OF RAT OR MOUSE POISON; BLEEDING FROM THE EARS, NOSE, OR MOUTH WITH ANY OF THE ABOVE SIGNS.

STEP 1: Examine for shock (see page 192). If the dog is weak and appears to be in shock, proceed to step 2 before transporting to the veterinarian.

STEP 2: Place the dog on its side with its head extended.

STEP 3: Gently pull out the dog's tongue to keep the airway open.

Step 3

STEP 4: Elevate the dog's hindquarters slightly by placing them on a pillow or folded towels.

STEP 5: To conserve body heat, place a hot water bottle (100°F/37°C) against the abdomen. Wrap the bottle in cloth to prevent burns.

Steps 4 and 5

STEP 6: Wrap the dog in a blanket or jacket.

STEP 7: Transport immediately to the veterinarian.

Step 6

135

BLEEDING:
Chest Or Abdomen

WATCH FOR SIGNS OF SHOCK: PALE OR WHITE GUMS, RAPID HEARTBEAT AND BREATHING. IF SIGNS ARE PRESENT, SEE PAGE 192.

STEP 1: Restrain the dog if necessary. See page 115.

STEP 2: If the wound is in the chest and a "sucking" noise is heard, bandage tightly enough to keep air from entering and transport immediately to the veterinarian. If not, proceed to Step 3.

STEP 3: If there is a protruding object, such as an arrow, see page 188.

Step 3

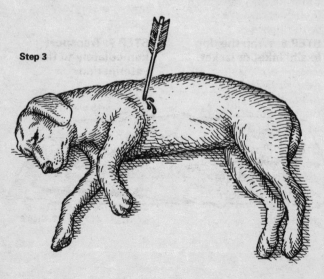

136

STEP 4: Clip the hair around the injured area.

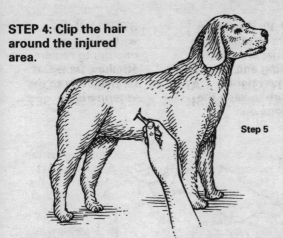

Step 5

STEP 5: Examine the wound for glass or other foreign objects. If visible, remove with fingers or tweezers. If the tissue under the wound appears to pass by when you move the skin, the wound will probably require stitches.

STEP 6: Flush thoroughly by pouring 3% hydrogen peroxide into wound. DO NOT use any other antiseptic.

STEP 7: Cover the wound with a clean cloth, sterile dressing, or a sanitary napkin.

STEP 8: Place your hand over the dressing and press firmly.

STEP 9: Keep pressure on the dressing to stop bleeding. If blood soaks through the dressing, DO NOT remove. Apply more dressing and continue to apply pressure until bleeding stops.

continued

STEP 10: Wrap torn sheets or other soft material around the dressing and tie or tape just tightly enough to keep the bandage on.

STEP 11: If the wound is deep enough to require stitches, transport immediately to the veterinarian.

Step 10

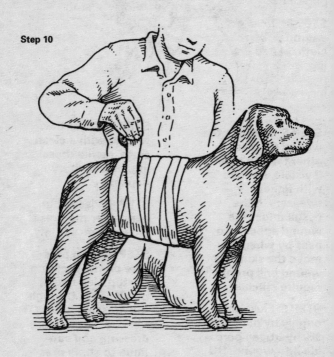

138

BLEEDING: Ear

> *Cut ears bleed profusely.*

STEP 1: Restrain the dog if necessary. See page 115.

Step 2

STEP 2: Cover the wound with a clean cloth, sterile dressing, or sanitary napkin. Place dressing material on both sides of the ear flap, then fold over the top of the dog's head and hold firmly to control bleeding.

Step 3

STEP 3: Wrap torn sheets or rags around the dressing, ear, and head, making sure the entire ear is covered. Tape or tie in place.

STEP 4: Transport immediately to the veterinarian.

BLEEDING: Leg, Paw, Or Tail

WATCH FOR SIGNS OF SHOCK: PALE OR WHITE GUMS, RAPID HEARTBEAT AND BREATHING. IF SIGNS ARE PRESENT, SEE PAGE 192.

STEP 1: Restrain the dog if necessary. See page 115.

STEP 2: Clip the hair around the injured area.

STEP 3: Examine the wound for glass or other foreign objects. If visible, remove with fingers or tweezers. If the tissue under the wound appears to pass by when you move the skin, the wound will probably require stitches.

Step 3

STEP 4: Flush thoroughly by pouring 3% hydrogen peroxide into the wound. DO NOT use any other antiseptic.

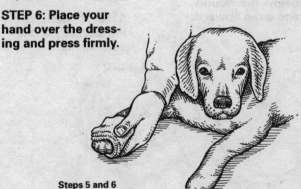

Step 4

STEP 5: Cover the wound with a clean cloth, sterile dressing, or a sanitary napkin.

STEP 6: Place your hand over the dressing and press firmly.

Steps 5 and 6

continued

STEP 7: Keep pressure on the dressing to stop bleeding. If blood soaks through the dressing, DO NOT remove. Apply more dressing and continue to apply pressure until bleeding stops. If bleeding does not stop within 5 minutes, proceed to Step 10.

STEP 8: Wrap torn rags or other soft material around the dressing and tie or tape just tightly enough to keep the bandage on. Start below the wound and wrap upward.

STEP 9: If the wound is deep enough to require stitches, keep the dog off the injured leg and transport immediately to the veterinarian.

STEP 10: If bleeding does not stop within 5 minutes, apply a tourniquet (see page 132).

STEP 11: If it will take time to reach the veterinarian, loosen the tourniquet every 15 minutes for a period of 1-2 minutes and then tighten again.

STEP 12: Transport immediately to the veterinarian.

Step 8

BLEEDING: Nail

A. NAIL BROKEN

STEP 1: Restrain the dog if necessary. See page 115.

STEP 2: DO NOT try to cut or remove the broken nail.

STEP 3: Push cake flour into exposed bleeding nail, then hold a clean cloth, sterile dressing, or sanitary napkin against the nail. Bleeding will stop in a few minutes.

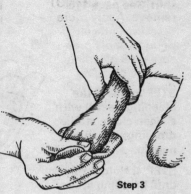

Step 3

STEP 4: Transport to the veterinarian as soon as possible.

B. NAIL CUT TOO SHORT

STEP 1: Restrain the dog if necessary. See page 115.

STEP 2: Push cake flour into exposed bleeding nail, then hold a clean cloth, sterile dressing, or sanitary napkin against the nail.

STEP 3: Keep firm pressure on the area for at least 5 min- utes. DO NOT remove until bleeding stops.

STEP 4: If bleeding does not stop in 15-20 minutes, transport to the veterinarian. Continuous bleeding indicates a bleeding disorder that should be treated promptly.

143

BLEEDING: Nose

STEP 1: Restrain the dog if necessary, but DO NOT tie its mouth shut. See page 115.

STEP 2: Apply ice packs to the top of the dog's nose between its eyes and nostrils.

Step 2

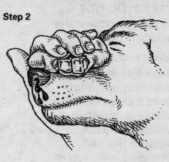

STEP 3: Cover the bleeding nostril with a clean cloth, sterile dressing, or sanitary napkin.

STEP 4: Hold firmly until bleeding stops.

STEP 5: If the nostril was not cut, a bloody nose in a dog could indicate a serious disorder. Transport to the veterinarian as soon as possible.

Step 3

Bloat

SIGNS: EXCESSIVE DROOLING, PACING AND AGITATION; ENLARGED ABDOMEN; FREQUENT ATTEMPTS TO VOMIT PRODUCING LARGE AMOUNTS OF WHITE FOAM OR NOTHING AT ALL. USUALLY SEEN IN LARGE, DEEP-CHESTED DOGS.

STEP 1: Transport immediately to the veterinarian. Bloat is frequently followed by gastric torsion (turning of the stomach), which leads to shock and death in a matter of a few hours.

BROKEN BONES: Back

SIGNS: PARALYSIS; UNUSUAL ARCH TO BACK; EXTREME PAIN IN BACK AREA.

WATCH FOR SIGNS OF SHOCK: PALE OR WHITE GUMS, RAPID HEARTBEAT AND BREATHING. IF SIGNS ARE PRESENT, SEE PAGE 192.

STEP 1: Restrain the dog if necessary. See page 115.

STEP 2: If you suspect a broken back, lift the dog onto a flat board without bending its back. DO NOT attempt to splint.

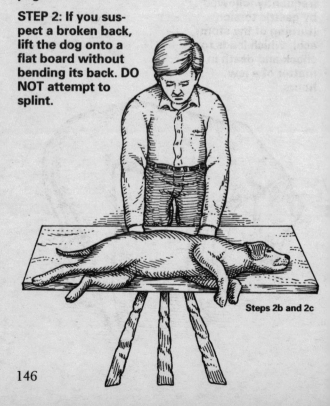

Steps 2b and 2c

a. Depending on the size of the dog, use a table leaf, ironing board, TV table top, large cutting board, or removable bookshelf. Make sure whatever you use will fit in your car.

b. Place two or three long strips of cloth or rope equidistant under the board.

c. Place one hand under the dog's chest and the other under its rear section and carefully lift or slide it onto the board.

d. Tie the dog onto the board.

STEP 3: Transport immediately to the veterinarian.

Step 2d

147

BROKEN BONES: Leg

SIGNS: LEG IS MISSHAPEN, HANGS LIMPLY, CANNOT SUPPORT BODY WEIGHT; SUDDEN ONSET OF PAIN IN AREA; SWELLING.

WATCH FOR SIGNS OF SHOCK: PALE OR WHITE GUMS, RAPID HEARTBEAT AND BREATHING. IF SIGNS ARE PRESENT, SEE PAGE 192.

STEP 1: Restrain the dog if necessary. See page 115.

STEP 2: Examine the leg and determine if the fracture is open (wound near the break or bone protruding from the skin) or closed (no break in the skin).

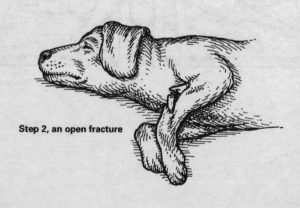

Step 2, an open fracture

STEP 3: If the fracture is closed, proceed to Step 4. If the fracture is open:

a. Flush thoroughly by pouring 3% hydrogen peroxide into the wound. DO NOT use any other antiseptic.

Step 3a

b. Cover the wound with a sterile bandage, clean cloth, or sanitary napkin.

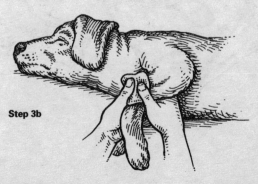

Step 3b

continued

149

c. DO NOT attempt
to splint the frac-
ture. Hold a
large folded
towel under the
unsplinted limb
and transport
immediately to
the veterinarian.

Step 3c

STEP 4: If the broken limb is grossly mis-shapen or the dog appears to be in great pain when you attempt to splint, stop and proceed to Step 5. Otherwise, proceed to splint the bone.

a. Use any splint material avail-able—sticks, newspaper, magazine, or stiff cardboard. The object is to immobilize the limb, not reset it.

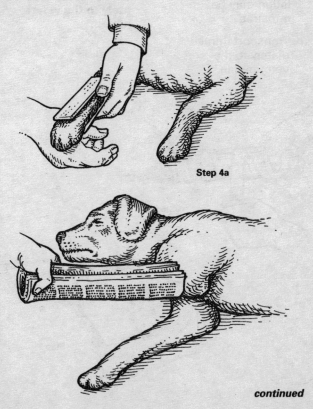

Step 4a

continued

b. Attach the splints to the fractured leg with torn strips of cloth or gauze.

c. Tape or tie firmly, but not so tightly that circulation may be impaired.

d. Transport immediately to the veterinarian.

STEP 5: If the broken limb is grossly misshapen or the dog appears to be in great pain when you attempt to splint, hold a large towel under the unsplinted limb for support and transport immediately to the veterinarian.

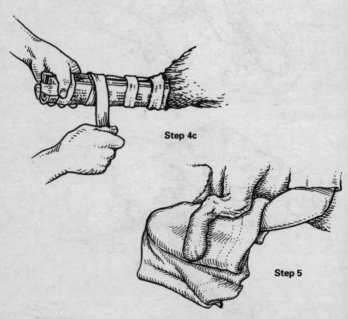

Step 4c

Step 5

BROKEN BONES: Ribs

SIGNS: UNUSUAL SHAPE OF RIB CAGE, EXTREME PAIN IN CHEST AREA.

WATCH FOR SIGNS OF SHOCK: PALE OR WHITE GUMS, RAPID HEARTBEAT AND BREATHING. IF SIGNS ARE PRESENT, SEE PAGE 192.

A. IF BROKEN RIBS ARE OBVIOUS OR SUSPECTED

STEP 1: Restrain the dog if necessary. See page 115.

STEP 2: Wrap torn sheets or gauze around the entire chest area to immobilize.

STEP 3: Transport immediately to the veterinarian.

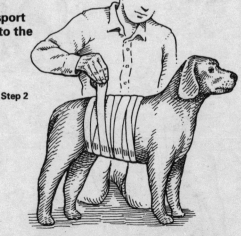

Step 2

continued

B. IF THE SIDE OF THE CHEST BULGES AS THE DOG BREATHES

> *A bulging chest usually means there is deep muscle damage to the chest wall that requires immediate professional attention.*

STEP 3: Bandage with torn cloth or gauze, tightly enough to keep pressure on the bulge.

STEP 4: Transport immediately to the veterinarian.

STEP 1: Restrain the dog if necessary. See page 115.

STEP 2: Cover the wound with a clean cloth, sterile dressing, or a sanitary napkin.

Step 2

Step 3

154

BURNS:
First Or Second Degree

SIGNS: 1ST DEGREE—FUR INTACT OR SINGED, PAINFUL LESION, SKIN RED WITH POSSIBLE BLISTERS. 2ND DEGREE— SINGED FUR, PAINFUL LESION WHICH TURNS DRY AND TAN IN COLOR, SWELLING.

STEP 1: Restrain the dog if necessary. See page 115.

STEP 2: Apply cold water or ice packs to the burned area and leave in contact with the skin for 15 minutes. DO NOT apply ointment or butter.

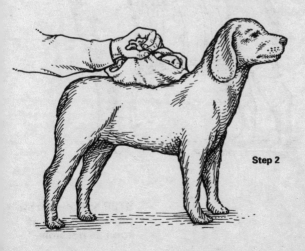

Step 2

continued

STEP 3: If burns cover a large part of the body or are located where the dog can lick them, cover with a sterile dressing. DO NOT use cotton.

STEP 4: Wrap torn rags or other soft material around the dressing and tie or tape just tightly enough to keep it in place.

Step 4

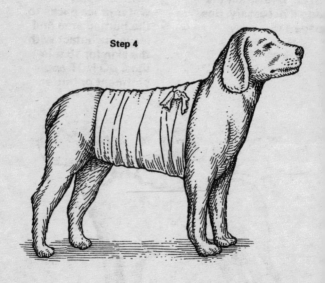

STEP 5: Transport to the veterinarian as soon as possible.

BURNS: Third Degree

SIGNS: PROBABLE SHOCK IF EXTENSIVE BODY AREA IS INVOLVED, DESTRUCTION OF ENTIRE SKIN AREA, BLACK OR PURE WHITE LESION, FUR PULLS OUT EASILY.

STEP 1: Restrain the dog if necessary. See page 115.

STEP 2: Examine for shock. See page 192.

STEP 3: Apply a dry, clean dressing over the burned area. DO NOT use cotton.

STEP 4: Wrap torn rags or other soft material around the dressing and tie or tape just tightly enough to keep it in place.

STEP 5: Transport to the veterinarian as soon as possible.

Step 4

BURNS: Chemical

SIGNS: CHEMICAL ODOR SUCH AS TURPENTINE, GASOLINE, OR INSECTICIDE; REDDENED SKIN; PAIN.

STEP 1: Restrain the dog if necessary. See page 115.

STEP 2: Wearing rubber gloves, wash the area thoroughly with mild soap or shampoo and water. Lather well and rinse thoroughly. Repeat as many times as necessary to remove the chemical. DO NOT use solvents of any kind.

STEP 3: Call the veterinarian for further instructions.

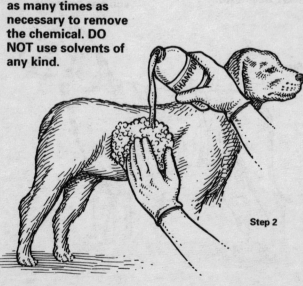

Step 2

Choking

SIGNS: PAWING AT MOUTH, PALE OR BLUE TONGUE, OBVIOUS DISTRESS, UNCONSCIOUSNESS.

STEP 1: Restrain the dog if necessary; DO NOT tie its mouth shut. See page 115.

STEP 2: Clear the airway.

a. Open the mouth carefully by grasping the upper jaw with one hand over the muzzle.

b. Press the lips over the upper teeth by pressing your thumb on one side and your fingers on the other so that the lips are between the dog's teeth and your fingers. Firm pressure will force the mouth open.

c. If you can see the object, try to remove it with your fingers.

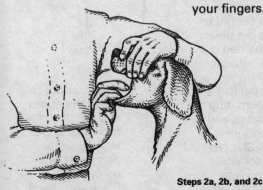

Steps 2a, 2b, and 2c

continued

159

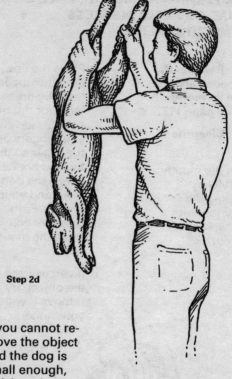

Step 2d

d. If you cannot re-move the object and the dog is small enough, pick it up by grasping its back legs; turn it up-side down and shake vigor-ously. Slapping the back while shaking may help to dislodge the object.

e. If you cannot re-move the object and the dog is too large to pick up, place the dog on its side on the floor. Place your hand just behind the

160

Step 2e

rib cage and press down and slightly forward quickly and firmly. Release. Repeat rapidly several times until the object is expelled.

STEP 3: If you cannot dislodge the object, transport immediately to the veterinarian.

STEP 4: If you dislodge the object and the dog is not breathing, feel for heartbeat by placing fingers about 2 inches behind the dog's elbow in the middle of its chest.

STEP 5: If the heart is not beating, proceed to Step 6. If it is, perform artificial respiration.

a. Turn the dog on its side.

b. Hold the dog's mouth and lips closed and blow firmly into its nostrils. Blow for 3 seconds, take a deep breath, and repeat until you feel resistance or see the chest rise.

c. After 1 minute, stop. Watch the chest for movement to indicate the dog is breathing on its own. *continued*

161

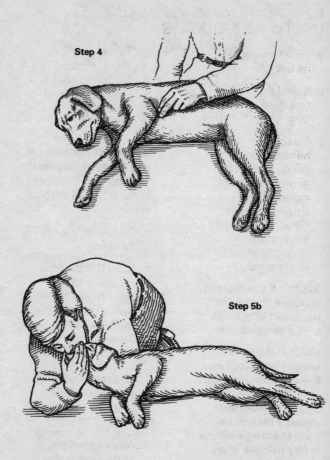

Step 4

Step 5b

d. If the dog is not breathing, continue artificial respiration.

STEP 6: If the heart is not beating, perform CPR (cardiopulmonary resuscitation).

CPR FOR DOGS WEIGHING UP TO 45 POUNDS

a. Turn the dog on its back.

b. Kneel down at the head of the dog.

c. Clasp your hands over the dog's chest with your palms resting on either side of its chest.

d. Compress your palms on the chest firmly for a count of "2" and release for a count of "1." Moderate pressure is required. Repeat about 30 times in 30 seconds (1 per second).

For dogs up to 45 pounds—Step 6c

e. Alternately (after 10 compressions), hold the dog's mouth and lips closed and blow firmly into its nostrils. Blow for 3 seconds, take a deep breath, and repeat until you feel resistance or see the chest rise. Try to repeat this 20 times in 60 seconds.

continued

f. After 1 minute, stop. Look at the chest for breathing movement and feel for heartbeat by placing fingers about 2 inches behind the dog's elbow in the center of its chest.

g. If the dog's heart is not beating, continue CPR. If the heart starts beating, but the dog is still not breathing, return to Step 5.

CPR FOR DOGS WEIGHING OVER 45 POUNDS

a. Turn the dog on its side.

b. Place the palm of your hand in the middle of the dog's chest.

c. Press for a count of "2" and release for a count of "1." Firm pressure is required. Repeat about 30 times in 30 seconds (1 per second).

d. Alternately (after 10 compressions), hold the dog's mouth and lips closed and blow firmly into its nostrils. Blow for 3 seconds, take a deep breath, and repeat until you feel resistance or see the chest rise. Try to repeat this 20 times in 60 seconds.

e. After 1 minute, stop. Look at the chest for breathing movement and feel for heartbeat by placing fingers about 2 inches behind the dog's elbow in the center of its chest.

**For dogs over 45
pounds—Step 6b**

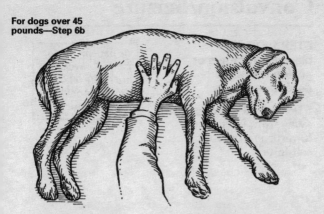

f. If the dog's heart
is not beating,
continue CPR. If
the heart starts
beating, but the
dog is still not
breathing, return
to Step 5.

**STEP 7: Transport
immediately to the
veterinarian. CPR or
artificial respiration
should be continued
on the way to the
veterinarian or until
dog is breathing and
its heart is beating
without assistance.**

**For dogs over 45
pounds—Step 6d**

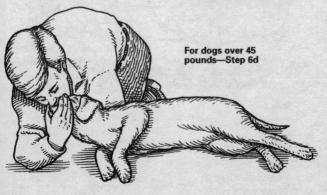

165

Convulsion/Seizure

STEP 1: DO NOT place your fingers or any object in the dog's mouth.

STEP 2: Pull the dog away from walls and furniture to prevent self-injury.

Be patient; do not panic. Convulsions are rarely fatal and most last only a few minutes.

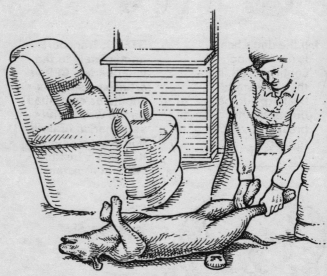

Step 2

STEP 3: Wrap the dog in a blanket to help protect it from injury.

STEP 4: When the seizure has stopped, contact the veterinarian for further instructions.

STEP 5: If the seizure does not stop within 10 minutes, or if the dog comes out of the seizure and goes into another one within an hour, transport immediately to the veterinarian.

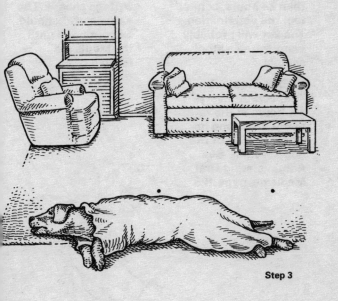

Step 3

Diarrhea

STEP 1: Remove all food immediately. Water is important to prevent dehydration in severe diarrhea. It should not be removed.

STEP 2: If blood appears or if diarrhea continues for more than 24 hours, contact the veterinarian. The vet will probably want to see a stool sample.

STEP 3: Treat with Kaopectate® every 4-6 hours at the rate of one teaspoon per 10-15 pounds of the dog's weight. See Administering Oral Medicine, page 125.

STEP 4: DO NOT attempt to feed for at least 12 hours.

STEP 5: After 12 hours, feed a bland diet consisting of small amounts of boiled ground beef, chicken, or lamb along with rice and cottage cheese. The Kaopectate® should be continued until the stools are formed.

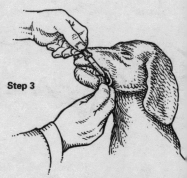

Step 3

Electrical Shock

WATCH FOR SIGNS OF SHOCK: PALE OR WHITE GUMS, RAPID HEARTBEAT AND BREATHING. IF SIGNS ARE PRESENT, SEE PAGE 192.

STEP 1: If the dog still has the electric cord in its mouth, DO NOT touch. First remove the plug from its outlet.

Step 1

continued

STEP 2: If the dog is unconscious, check for breathing. If the dog is conscious or breathing, proceed to Step 6. If the dog is not breathing, feel for heartbeat by placing fingers about 2 inches behind the elbow in the middle of its chest.

STEP 3: If the heart is not beating, proceed to Step 4. If it is, perform artificial respiration (see page 161).

STEP 4: If the heart is not beating, perform CPR (see page 162).

STEP 5: Transport immediately to the veterinarian. CPR or artificial respiration should be continued on the way to the veterinarian or until the dog is breathing and its heart is beating without assistance.

STEP 6: If the dog's mouth or lips are burned (bright red), swab them gently with 3% hydrogen peroxide.

Step 2

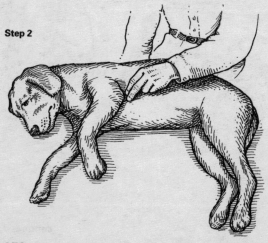

STEP 7: To conserve body heat, place a hot water bottle (100°F/37°C) against the dog's abdomen. Wrap the bottle in cloth to prevent burns. Wrap the dog in a blanket or jacket.

STEP 8: Transport immediately to the veterinarian.

Step 6

Step 7

171

EYE INJURIES:
Eyeball Out Of Socket

Minutes are
important in
saving the eye.

**STEP 1: Restrain the
dog if necessary. See
page 115.**

**STEP 2: Hold a clean,
wet towel over the
eye.**

**STEP 3: Transport
immediately to the
veterinarian.**

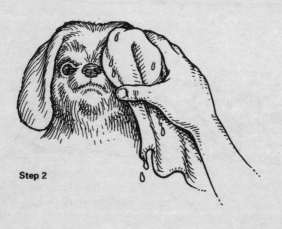

Step 2

EYE INJURIES:
Object In Eye

STEP 1: DO NOT try to remove the object.

STEP 2: Restrain the dog if necessary. See page 115.

STEP 3: Prevent self-injury to the eye.

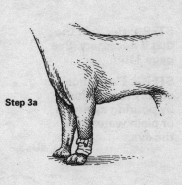

Step 3a

a. Dewclaws (if present) should be bandaged on the front paw on the same side as the affected eye.

b. For small dogs, cut a large piece of cardboard into an Elizabethan-type collar.

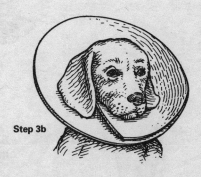

c. For larger dogs, cut the bottom from a plastic bucket, fit the bucket over the dog's head, and hold it in place by tying it to the dog's collar.

Step 3b

STEP 4: Transport immediately to the veterinarian.

EYE INJURIES: Scratched Or Irritated Eye

SIGNS: SQUINTING, RUBBING OR PAWING AT EYES; THICK DISCHARGE OR REDNESS.

STEP 1: Restrain the dog if necessary. See page 115.

STEP 2: Flush thoroughly (3 or 4 times) by pouring eyewash or plain water into the eye.

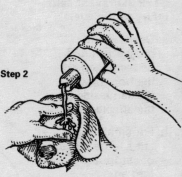

Step 2

Step 3a

STEP 3: Prevent self-injury to the eye.

a. Dewclaws (if present) should be bandaged on the front paw on the same side as the affected eye.

174

b. For small dogs, cut a large piece of cardboard into an Elizabethan-type collar.

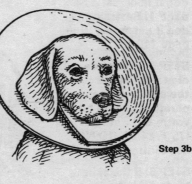

c. For larger dogs, cut the bottom from a plastic bucket, fit the bucket over the dog's head, and hold it in place by tying it to the dog's collar.

STEP 4: Transport immediately to the veterinarian.

Step 3b

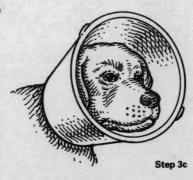

Step 3c

175

Frostbite

SIGNS: PAIN, PALE SKIN IN EARLY STAGES, RED OR BLACK SKIN IN ADVANCED STAGES.

CAUTION: FROSTBITE CAN BE PAINFUL. HANDLE ANIMAL WITH CARE!

STEP 1: Restrain the dog if necessary. See page 115.

STEP 2: Warm the area with moist towels. Water temperature should be warm but not hot (75°F/24°C). DO NOT use ointment.

STEP 3: If the skin turns dark, transport to the veterinarian as soon as possible.

The most commonly affected areas are the ears and tail tip.

Step 2

Heatstroke

**SIGNS: EXCESSIVE DROOLING, LACK OF
COORDINATION, RAPID BREATHING, TOP
OF THE HEAD HOT TO THE TOUCH.**

STEP 1: Remove the
dog from the hot
environment.

STEP 2: Immerse the
dog in a cold water
bath or continuously
run a garden hose on
its body; continue
either treatment for
at least 30 minutes.

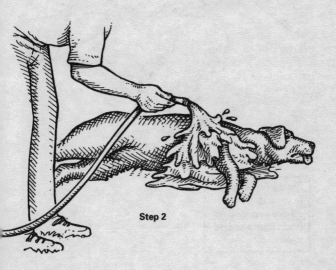

Step 2

continued

STEP 3: Apply ice packs to the top of the head; keep them there while transporting to the veterinarian.

STEP 4: Transport to the veterinarian immediately after the above treatment.

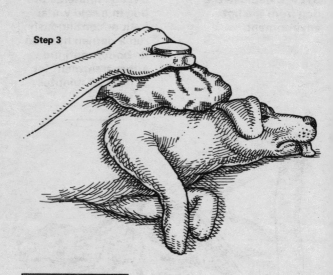

Step 3

> *Prompt treatment is urgent. Heatstroke can lead to brain damage and death.*

Hypothermia

SIGNS: DEPRESSION, SUBNORMAL BODY TEMPERATURE, COMA.

STEP 1: Warm the dog.

a. Place a hot water bottle (100°F/37°C) against the dog's abdomen. Wrap the bottle in cloth to prevent burns. Wrap the dog in a blanket or jacket. OR

b. Use a heating pad; keep the setting on "low" and turn the dog every few minutes to prevent burns.

STEP 2: Transport immediately to the veterinarian.

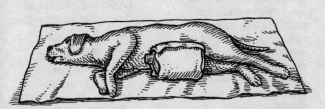

Step 1a

POISONING: Corrosive Or Petroleum-Base

SIGNS: BURNS ON MOUTH IF CORROSIVE, CHARACTERISTIC ODOR IF PETROLEUM PRODUCT, SEVERE ABDOMINAL PAIN, VOMITING, DIARRHEA, BLOODY URINE, COMA.

WATCH FOR SIGNS OF SHOCK: PALE OR WHITE GUMS, RAPID HEARTBEAT AND BREATHING. IF SIGNS ARE PRESENT, SEE PAGE 192.

Corrosives include battery acid, corn and callous remover, dishwasher detergent, drain cleaner, grease remover, lye, and oven cleaner. Petroleum products include paint solvent, floor wax, and dry cleaning-solution. If in doubt as to type of poison, call the veterinarian or Poison Control Center.

STEP 1: If the dog is comatose or convulsing, wrap it in a blanket and transport immediately to the veterinarian.

If the dog is not comatose or convulsing, proceed to Step 2.

STEP 2: Restrain the dog if necessary. See page 115.

STEP 3: Flush the dog's mouth and muzzle thoroughly with large amounts of water. Make sure its head is at a slight downward angle so it does not choke.

STEP 4: DO NOT induce vomiting. Give 1 tablespoon of olive oil or egg white.

Step 3

a. If necessary, apply a mouth-tie loosely to limit jaw movement. See page 116.

b. Tip the dog's head slightly backward.

c. Pull the lower lip out at the corner to make a pouch.

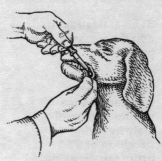

Steps 4c and 4d

d. Place the fluid slowly into the pouch a little at a time, allowing each small amount to be swallowed before giving any more of the dose.

e. Gently rub the throat to stimulate swallowing.

STEP 5: Take the dog and container of the suspected poison to the veterinarian immediately.

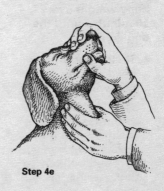

Step 4e

181

POISONING: Noncorrosive

SIGNS: EXCESSIVE DROOLING, VOMITING, ABDOMINAL PAIN, LACK OF COORDINATION.

WATCH FOR SIGNS OF SHOCK: PALE OR WHITE GUMS, RAPID HEARTBEAT AND BREATHING. IF SIGNS ARE PRESENT, SEE PAGE 192.

STEP 1: Restrain the dog if necessary. See page 115.

STEP 2: If the dog has not already vomited, induce vomiting immediately by giving 1 teaspoon of 3% hydrogen peroxide per 10 pounds of body weight every 10 minutes until the dog vomits.

a. Tip the dog's head slightly backward.

b. Pull the lower lip out at the corner to make a pouch.

c. Using a plastic eyedropper or dose syringe, place the fluid slowly into the pouch a little at a time. Allow each small amount to be swallowed before giving any more of the dose.

d. Gently rub the throat to stimulate swallowing.

STEP 3: If no 3% hydrogen peroxide is available, place a heaping teaspoon of table salt in the back of the dog's mouth every 10 minutes until the dog vomits.

a. Grasp the upper jaw with one hand over the muzzle.

b. Press the lips over the upper teeth by pressing your thumb on one side and your fingers on the other so the dog's lips are between its teeth and your fingers. Firm pressure will force the mouth open.

c. Holding the tea-spoon of salt in the other hand, place the salt as far back in the mouth as possible.

d. Gently rub the throat to stimulate swallowing.

STEP 4: Save the vomit material for the veterinarian.

STEP 5: Take the dog, vomit, and container of suspected poison to the veterinarian immediately.

Steps 3a, 3b, and 3c

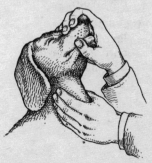

Step 3d

183

POISONING: Plants

SIGNS: DROOLING, VOMITING, DIARRHEA, ABDOMINAL PAIN, LACK OF COORDINATION.

STEP 1: Restrain the dog if necessary. See page 115.

STEP 2: If the dog has not already vomited, induce vomiting immediately by giving 1 teaspoon of 3% hydrogen peroxide per 10 pounds of body weight every 10 minutes until the dog vomits.

a. Tip the dog's head slightly backward.

b. Pull the lower lip out at the corner to make a pouch.

c. Using a plastic eyedropper or dose syringe, place the fluid slowly into the pouch a little at a time. Allow each small amount to be swallowed before giving any more of the dose.

d. Gently rub the throat to stimulate swallowing.

See list of poisonous plants on page 51. It is safe to assume that all common houseplants are toxic to some degree.

STEP 3: If no 3% hydrogen peroxide is available, place a heaping teaspoon of table salt in the back of the dog's mouth every 10 minutes until the dog vomits.

a. Grasp the upper jaw with one hand over the muzzle.

b. Press the lips over the upper teeth by pressing your thumb on one side and your fingers on the other so the dog's lips are between its teeth and your fingers. Firm pressure will force the mouth open.

c. Holding the tea-spoon of salt in the other hand, place the salt as far back in the mouth as possible.

d. Gently rub the throat to stimulate swallowing.

STEP 4: If convulsions or difficulty in breathing develop, take the dog and a leaf of the suspected plant to the veterinarian immediately.

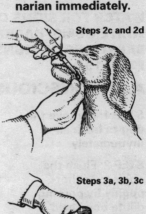

Steps 2c and 2d

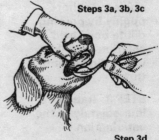

Steps 3a, 3b, 3c

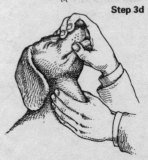

Step 3d

185

POISONING: Smoke Or Carbon Monoxide Inhalation

SIGNS: DEPRESSION, LACK OF COORDINATION, HEAVY PANTING, DEEP RED GUMS, POSSIBLE CONVULSIONS.

WATCH FOR SIGNS OF SHOCK: PALE OR WHITE GUMS, RAPID HEARTBEAT AND BREATHING. IF SIGNS ARE PRESENT, SEE PAGE 192.

A. IF CONSCIOUS

STEP 1: Remove the dog to fresh air immediately.

STEP 2: Flush the dog's eyes thoroughly by pouring dilute boric acid solution or plain water directly into them.

STEP 3: Transport immediately to the veterinarian.

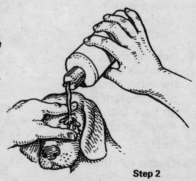

Step 2

B. IF UNCONSCIOUS

STEP 1: Remove the dog to fresh air immediately.

STEP 2: If the dog is not breathing, feel for heartbeat by placing fingers about 2 inches behind the dog's elbow in the middle of its chest.

STEP 3: If the heart is not beating, proceed to Step 4. If it is, perform artificial respiration (see page 161).

STEP 4: If the heart is not beating, perform CPR (see page 162).

STEP 5: Transport immediately to the veterinarian. CPR or artificial respiration should be continued on the way to the veterinarian or until the dog is breathing and its heart is beating without assistance.

Step 2

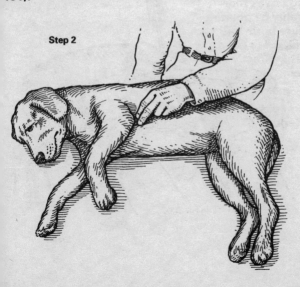

187

Puncture Wound

WATCH FOR SIGNS OF SHOCK: PALE OR WHITE GUMS, RAPID HEARTBEAT AND BREATHING. IF SIGNS ARE PRESENT, SEE PAGE 192.

A. IF THE OBJECT (KNIFE, ARROW, STICK, ETC.) IS PROTRUDING

STEP 1: Restrain the dog if necessary, taking care not to touch the object. See page 115.

STEP 2: DO NOT attempt to remove the object.

STEP 3: Place clean cloths, sterile dressings, or sanitary napkins around the point of entry.

Step 3

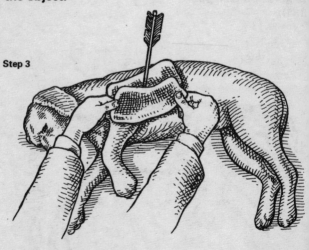

STEP 4: Bandage tightly around the point of entry.

STEP 5: Transport immediately to the veterinarian.

Step 4

B. OTHER PUNCTURE WOUNDS

STEP 1: Restrain the dog if necessary. See page 115.

STEP 2: If the wound is in the chest and a "sucking" noise is heard, bandage tightly enough to seal the wound and transport immediately to the veterinarian.

Step 2

continued

189

STEP 3: Clip the hair around the wound.

STEP 4: Examine the wound carefully for foreign objects such as glass or wood splinters. If present, remove with tweezers or needle-nose pliers.

Step 3

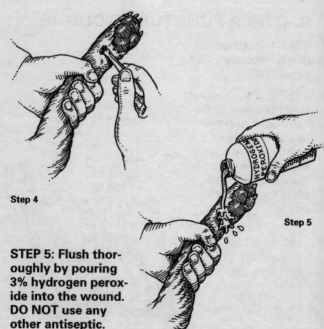

Step 4

Step 5

STEP 5: Flush thoroughly by pouring 3% hydrogen peroxide into the wound. DO NOT use any other antiseptic.

190

STEP 6: DO NOT bandage. Allow the wound to drain unless there is excessive bleeding. If the wound DOES bleed excessively:

a. Cover the wound with a clean cloth, sterile dressing, or sanitary napkin.

b. Place your hand over the dressing and press firmly.

c. Keep pressure on the dressing to stop bleeding. If blood soaks through the dressing, DO NOT remove. Apply more dressing and continue to apply pressure until bleeding stops. If bleeding does not stop within 5 minutes, proceed to Step 7.

d. Wrap torn rags or other soft material around the dressing and tie or tape just tightly enough to keep the bandage in place.

STEP 7: If bleeding does not stop within 5 minutes, apply a tourniquet (see page 132). DO NOT apply a tourniquet to the head or torso.

STEP 8: If it will take time to reach the veterinarian, loosen the tourniquet every 15 minutes for a period of 1-2 minutes and then tighten again.

STEP 9: Transport immediately to the veterinarian.

Step 6d

191

Shock

SIGNS: PALE OR WHITE GUMS, VERY FAST HEARTBEAT (OVER 150 BEATS PER MINUTE), RAPID BREATHING.

Any trauma or serious injury can cause shock. If the dog is in shock, do not take time to splint fractures or treat minor injuries.

STEP 1: Examine for shock.

a. Examine the gums by gently lifting the upper lip so the gum is visible. Pale or white gums indicate the dog is almost certainly in shock and may have serious internal injuries and/or bleeding. If the gums are pink, the dog is probably not in shock.

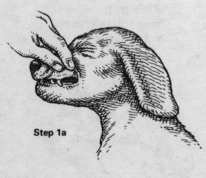

Step 1a

b. Determine the heartbeat. Place fingers firmly on the dog's chest about 2 inches behind the dog's elbow in the center of its chest (see illustration on page 162). Count the number of beats in 10 seconds and multiply by 6. If the dog is in shock, its heartbeat may be over 150 beats per minute.

STEP 2: Place dog on its side with its head extended.

STEP 3: Gently pull out the dog's tongue to keep the airway open.

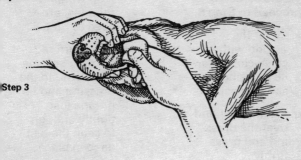

Step 3

STEP 4: Elevate the dog's hindquarters slightly by placing them on a pillow or folded towels.

Step 4

continued

STEP 5: Stop visible bleeding immediately; if blood is spurting and the wound is on the leg or tail, proceed to Step 6. If there is no visible bleeding, proceed to Step 8.

a. Cover the wound with a clean cloth, sterile dressing, or sanitary napkin.

b. Place your hand over the dressing and press firmly.

c. Keep pressure on the dressing to stop bleeding. If blood soaks through the dressing, DO NOT remove.

Apply more dressing and continue to apply pressure until bleeding stops. If bleeding does not stop within 5 minutes, proceed to Step 6.

d. Wrap torn rags or other soft material around the dressing and tie or tape just tightly enough to keep the bandage in place.

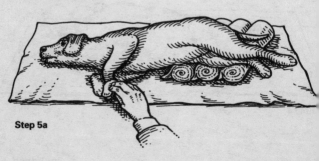

Step 5a

STEP 6: If bleeding does not stop within 5 minutes or if blood is spurting, apply a tourniquet (see page 132). DO NOT apply a tourniquet to the head or torso.

STEP 7: If it will take time to reach the veterinarian, loosen the tourniquet every 15 minutes for a period of 1-2 minutes and then tighten again.

STEP 8: To conserve body heat, place a hot water bottle (100°F/37°C) against the abdomen. Wrap the bottle in cloth to prevent burns. Wrap the dog in a blanket or jacket.

STEP 9: Transport immediately to the veterinarian.

Step 8

195

Skunk Encounter

STEP 1: Restrain the dog if necessary. See page 115.

STEP 2: Flush the dog's eyes with fresh water.

STEP 3: Remove and destroy leather collars or harnesses.

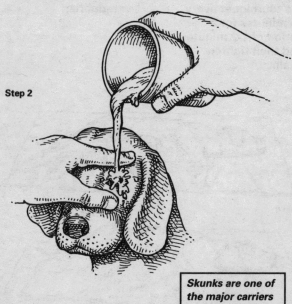

Step 2

Skunks are one of the major carriers of rabies in North America.

STEP 4: Bathe the dog thoroughly with soap or shampoo and water.

STEP 5: Apply plain tomato juice liberally. After several minutes, bathe again with soap or shampoo and water. Time will eventually remove the odor. Skunk odor neutralizers are available.

STEP 6: If the skunk is destroyed, take it to the veterinarian for a rabies examination. DO NOT touch the skunk with your bare hands.

STEP 7: If the dog is not currently vaccinated for rabies, contact the veterinarian.

Step 4

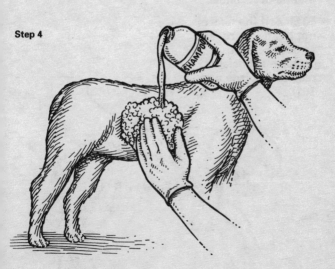

197

Unconsciousness

STEP 1: If you suspect choking, see page 159.

STEP 2: If the dog is breathing, check for shock. See page 192. If the dog is not breathing, proceed to Step 3.

STEP 3: Feel for heartbeat by placing fingers about 2 inches behind the dog's elbow in the middle of its chest.

STEP 4: If the heart is not beating, proceed to Step 5. If it is, perform artificial respiration (see page 161).

STEP 5: If the heart is not beating, perform CPR (see page 162).

STEP 6: Transport immediately to the veterinarian. CPR or artificial respiration should be continued on the way to the veterinarian or until the dog is breathing and its heart is beating without assistance.

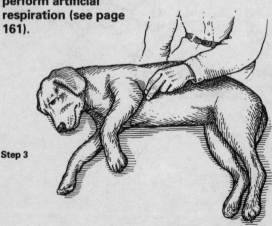

Step 3

Vomiting

STEP 1: Remove all food and water immediately.

STEP 2: If vomiting contains blood or is frequent, contact the veterinarian immediately. If not, proceed to Step 3.

STEP 3: Treat with Pepto-Bismol® every 4 hours at the rate of 1 teaspoon per 10-15 pounds of the dog's weight. See Administering Oral Medicine, page 125.

STEP 4: DO NOT attempt to feed or give water for at least 12 hours.

STEP 5: After 12 hours, feed a bland diet consisting of small amounts of boiled ground beef, chicken, or lamb along with rice and cottage cheese. If this is held down, a transition to regular diet should take place over the next two days by mixing an increasing quantity of regular dog food with the bland mixture.

The Whys Of Emergency Treatment

Restraining An Injured Dog

If the dog is conscious, you must get close enough to it to look it over carefully. But an injured dog is usually frightened and in pain, and unless it feels very secure with your presence, it may try to escape or even bite you. Therefore, approach it slowly, stoop down to the dog's level, and talk in a reassuring tone.

You can tell a great deal about how the dog will react to you by observing its eyes and facial expression. If the dog is very submissive, it will show this by having its head slightly lowered, the mouth drawn back a little into what appears to be a smile.

First, slowly attempt to pet it under the jaw. If this is accepted, then pet the top of its head while continuing to talk reassuringly. It is best not to take chances, so slip a length of rope around its neck, and then apply a muzzle. At this point, you can examine it thoroughly and then treat the injuries.

If the dog is growling and its eyes are dilated, do not attempt to touch it. Continue to talk reassuringly, but try to slip a rope over its head and around its neck. Following this with a muzzle is necessary before you can attempt to examine it. Your goal is to ease the dog's suffering and stabilize its vital signs quickly before transporting to a vet.

Transporting An Injured Dog

Try not to move an injured dog more than necessary, and get it to a veterinarian as soon as possible. Have someone call the veterinarian to be certain he or she is prepared for your arrival.

Depending on the injury, wrap the dog in blankets or use a blanket or flat board as a stretcher. If you suspect a broken back, a stiff board of some kind must be used. Before you move the dog, make sure the board will fit into your car. Then move it next to the dog, put the ties underneath the board, and gently lift or slide the dog onto it. Fasten the ties over the dog to hinder movement.

If the dog is not breathing and/or its heart is not beating, the dog will certainly die or may be dead already. CPR should be continued on the way to the veterinarian. It cannot hurt, and many people give up trying too early.

Animal Bite

When a dog gets into a fight with another dog, a cat, or a wild animal, damage can occur to both the skin and the underlying tissue. Many dog fights can be avoided by not letting your dog run loose. The dog should also be trained to obey your commands.

If your dog does get into a fight, do not try to break it up with your bare hands. A fighting dog will bite anything, including you. Pull your leashed dog out of harm's way or use a long stick.

When the fight is over, examine your dog carefully for hidden wounds. You'll often find punctures around the neck area and on the legs. Look through the hair carefully to find bloodstains, which would indicate the skin has been punctured.

After clipping the hair from around the wound to assess the damage, flush with 3% hydrogen peroxide to prevent infection. This is one of the major complications of a bite.

The dog should then be seen by a veterinarian. Although there may be only a few punctures, extensive damage may have been done to underlying muscles through the pressure of the bite. If the wounds are deep enough to require stitches, this should be done immediately by a professional.

Unless there is extensive bleeding, the wounds should be left open to drain until the dog is seen by the veterinarian. Whenever tissue is damaged, fluid accumulates in the area. If the wound is not left open to drain, a painful swelling will occur and the site becomes a perfect medium for the growth of bacteria and infection. Tetanus is quite rare in dogs, but it is possible. The decision to inoculate should be left to your veterinarian.

It is important to determine if the biting animal has been inoculated against rabies. If the biter is a wild animal such as a skunk or raccoon, efforts should be made to destroy it so the brain can be examined for rabies. Never touch the animal with your bare hands, even after it has been killed. Wear gloves or wrap the body in a blanket. Your veterinarian will take care of the rabies examination.

Bleeding

With a bleeding injury, the main purpose of first aid is to prevent excessive blood loss, which can lead to shock. Pressure is applied to the wound to allow the normal clotting mechanism of the blood to stop the leak. This is a complex process, but basically, the blood cells form a fine screen over the wound and thus prevent further loss of blood. That is why it is important not to remove the dressing once it has been applied. If you lift it to look at the wound, you will break up the clots that are forming and the wound will continue to bleed.

If the wound continues to bleed through the dressing, it will be necessary to use a tourniquet. The tourniquet should be used only as a last resort, because it not only stops the bleeding, it also prevents blood from getting to other tissues in the area, which become oxygen starved and die.

Blood is carried away from the heart by the arteries and returned by the veins. If an artery is cut, the blood will spurt with each beat of the heart. Cut arteries require immediate care to stop the bleeding and usually require veterinary care for repair.

The paws and legs of a dog are vulnerable to injury from broken glass, nails, etc. The multiple blood vessels are close to the skin surface and are easily cut when the skin is injured. This is why the paws and legs bleed so heavily when injured.

An injured ear will also bleed heavily because the skin over the ear is so thin. A dog's reaction to an injured ear is usually to shake its head, which makes things worse. By taping the ear over the head, you combat the pull of gravity and thus give the blood a better chance to clot. Firm bandaging is necessary to accomplish this.

Nails cause considerable problems to dog owners. Frequently the nails break because they get caught in ground crevices or simply break when the dog is exercising on rough ground. Clipping the nails too short is another frequent cause of bleeding. It is important to remember that nails will eventually stop bleeding if the treatment suggested in the First Aid portion of this book is followed, unless the dog has a disease which prevents clotting. In this case, it should be seen at once by a veterinarian.

In the center of each nail is a blood vessel and a nerve. This is seen as the pink area in white nails but is impossible to see on black nails, which makes them very difficult to cut. If you cut your dog's nails yourself, it is important not to cut into this "quick," as it is called, but to clip the nail just in front of it. If the "quick" is cut, the nail will bleed and the cut nerve will cause some pain. If the dog is nervous and upset, have a professional cut the nails for you. Frequent cutting will allow the blood vessel and nerve to move further back into the nail and thus allow you to cut the nail shorter.

Bloat

It is hard to accept the fact that a seemingly healthy dog can, within an hour, be fighting for its life. Bloat is an extremely serious, potentially fatal condition. Professional treatment is urgent and should not be delayed. Bloat can lead to death within a very short period of time. It seems to affect large, deep-chested dogs most.

The symptoms are dramatic. The animal is usually frantically trying to vomit, but can produce nothing but thick, white mucus. The abdomen directly behind the ribs swells enormously and, when tapped with your fingers, sounds like a drum.

We have no satisfactory scientific explanation as to why bloat occurs. Basically, the stomach fills with gas, like a blown-up balloon. But with the balloon, there is room for expansion. With the stomach, there is none, so the gas places pressure on the spleen, liver, and other organs. The result can be shock and death in a short period of time.

We do know that excessive fermentation of food occurs in the stomach. There are apparently some toxic by-products of this fermentation that prevent release of gas buildup by the normal means of belching or passing the gas into the intestines. The bloated animal can do neither, and without immediate release of this pressure, death occurs.

Bloat is frequently followed by gastric torsion— that is, the stomach turns on itself. If this occurs, certain death will follow unless swift professional help is obtained.

To prevent bloat and subsequent torsion, feed the dog small meals several times a day rather than one large meal, and see that heavy exercise is avoided after meals.

Broken Bones

With dogs, as with human beings, all bones are subject to breakage, but leg fractures are by far the most common. It is important to remember that dogs have a high pain tolerance and often a dangling leg seems to cause no pain. Therefore, don't be afraid to handle the fractured limb (gently!). The dog will let you know if it hurts. If the dog is in pain or if the fracture is open, do not attempt to splint. Simply clean the wound, then hold a towel under the limb for support and transport to a vet.

An open fracture is one where the bone is protruding or there is a break in the skin over the broken bone. First aid efforts should be directed to the control of infection, since the exposed bone is subject to bacterial invasion. Proper cleaning is of prime importance. Use only 3% hydrogen peroxide to clean the wound. Other antiseptics may cause tissue damage.

A closed fracture is one with the bone broken but the skin intact. The leg should be splinted, but do not confuse splinting with setting the limb, which should be done by a professional. Splinting is only a temporary procedure, so you may use any firm material at hand. The purpose of a splint is to prevent further damage by immobilizing the limb and to make the animal more comfortable during the trip to the veterinarian.

Burns

Burns can be caused by fire, heat, boiling liquids, chemicals, and electricity. All are painful and can cause damage, even death. Most scalds can be avoided by care in the kitchen. Because the dog is often underfoot while its owner is cooking, care should be taken when handling hot water or oil.

Superficial burns, evidenced by pain and reddening of the skin, are usually not serious. However, first aid should be given as soon as possible to ease the pain. Burns tend to "cook" the skin, and in order to stop this cooking process, cold water or ice packs (not butter or grease) should be applied to the burned area at once.

Third degree burns are far more serious. Depending on how much of the body is involved, they can cause death. The deeper the layers of skin involved, the more likely the dog is to go into shock. The outer skin layers are destroyed and the unprotected lower layers are then susceptible to infection. If the burns are extensive, a great deal of fluid from the tissue cells will be lost, and shock is certain to result. Therefore, treatment for shock is your first priority and should be continued until professional help can be obtained.

Chemical burns can also endanger our pets. Such products as drain cleaner or paint thinner can cause serious skin damage, and poisoning if ingested. To prevent accidents of this nature, all such products should be kept out of the dog's reach.

If you notice a chemical odor on your dog, often the first sign of this type of burn, bathe it immediately. Do not use solvents of any kind on the skin. Use mild soap and lather well; rinse thoroughly until the odor has disappeared.

Unlike with heat burns, a soothing antibiotic can then be applied to the affected area until the dog can be treated by a vet. Be sure all the chemical is removed before the ointment is applied.

Electrical burns are most often caused by chewing on an electrical cord. The burns are almost always located on both sides of the mouth or lips. Most of these burns are minor and will heal nicely if kept clean with 3% hydrogen peroxide. Electro-cution is the far more serious effect of chewing on the cord. If you have a young puppy or if your dog tends to chew anything in sight, do not leave it alone where cords are within its reach.

Choking

When a dog is choking on a foreign object, it needs help at once. The harder it tries to breathe, the more panicky it becomes. Your goal is to open the airway without being bitten. If you cannot reach the object with your fingers, or if the dog is struggling too much to let you try, turn the dog upside down and shake it. This will often dislodge the object and propel it out of the mouth.

Of course, a different method must be used with a larger dog. The abdominal compression tech-nique can be compared to pushing the air out of a beach ball. The sudden thrusts on the abdomen cause the diaphragm to bulge forward into the chest. This in turn forces air, and frequently the object, out of the windpipe.

If the dog is unconscious and you believe a foreign object is present, you must open the airway before giving artificial respiration or cardiac mas-sage. If the dog cannot breathe, efforts to revive it will be fruitless.

The method of artificial respiration presented here is the most effective. Blowing directly into the dog's nostrils inflates the lungs to the fullest and the result is maximum oxygenation.

Cardiac massage keeps the blood pumping through the vessels and stimulates the heart muscle to contract and start beating again. With smaller dogs, you compress the heart by actually squeezing it. This keeps the blood pressure up and starts normal heart muscle contractions.

The same results are achieved with larger dogs by a different method. The chest is usually too large to compress effectively between your hands, so only one hand is used, and the chest is compressed against the floor.

The purpose of artificial respiration and cardiac massage is to keep oxygenated blood circulating to the brain. If the brain does not receive this oxygenated blood, the dog will die.

CPR (cardiopulmonary resuscitation) is a combination of artificial respiration and cardiac massage. It should be continued until the dog is breathing well by itself, or until you can get it to a veterinarian. It should be continued on the way. Your continued efforts may save the dog's life.

Convulsion/Seizure

A convulsion or seizure is rarely fatal, but it is a frightening experience when seen for the first time. It is the result of constant electrical firing of the muscles of the body from the brain.

It is important not to panic. You are not in danger, but the dog needs help to protect it from self-injury. Pull it away from walls and furniture and, if possible, wrap it in a blanket.

Do not attempt to place anything in the dog's mouth. This will not help the dog and you may be bitten. The dog is not aware of its actions during the seizure, which usually lasts only a few minutes.

This is followed by 15 minutes to a half hour of recovery time, during which period the dog may be dazed and confused.

Not all seizures are due to simple epilepsy. Some are caused by lead or other poisons, liver diseases, and even brain tumors. Seizures or convulsions should never be taken lightly. The problem should be discussed with a veterinarian as soon as possible.

Diarrhea

Diarrhea is a commonly encountered problem that occurs when food is passed through the intestine too rapidly. It can be caused by allergies, milk, worms, or spoiled food. There are also more serious causes such as tumors, viral infections, and diseases of the liver, pancreas, and kidney.

Initial home treatment should be conservative. Food should be withheld for 12 hours, but water should be available as frequent diarrhea can cause dehydration. Kaopectate® is beneficial because it coats the irritated intestinal surfaces.

The first meal should consist of a bland diet consisting of small amounts of boiled ground beef, chicken, or lamb along with rice and cottage cheese. The Kaopectate® should be continued until the stools are normal.

It is important to seek professional help if blood, severe depression, or abdominal pain are present.

Electrical Shock

Grown dogs are seldom victims of electrical shocks. But puppies are naturally curious and will chew almost anything, including electrical cords. If the insulation is punctured and the mouth comes in contact with both wires, the dog will receive a shock and may be unable to release the cord.

You must disconnect the cord from the socket immediately, before touching the dog. If you touch the dog before disconnecting the cord, you could be electrocuted.

Once the cord is disconnected, you can safely touch the dog. Examine it carefully. Electrocution can cause severe heart damage and fluid accumulation in the lungs. Strong shock can stop the heart, and CPR must be performed immediately to start the heart beating again.

Often the mouth will be burned from contact with the bare wires. These burns look much more serious than they are and will heal eventually if cleaned and treated properly.

Most electrical shocks require professional attention and the victim should be taken to the veterinarian immediately.

Eye Injuries

Irritation of the eye can be caused by allergies, dust and dirt, lashes growing inward, fights, etc. It can result in a mild inflammation of the tissue around the eye or severe damage to the cornea.

When examining the eye, it is important to know that dogs have a third eyelid located in the corner of the eye nearest the nose. This third eyelid can completely cover the eyeball and sometimes gives the appearance that part of the eye is gone. In addition to being a protective mechanism, it can also indicate that something is wrong with the eye.

If it is raised and looks red, the eye is inflamed. Do not try to touch or manipulate this eyelid.

Other indications that the eye is irritated are squinting as well as rubbing and pawing at the eye. Your first priority is to prevent self-injury since this often causes more severe damage than the original irritation.

Flat-nosed breeds with protruding eyes, such as pugs and Pekinese, are more susceptible to eye irritations than long-nosed breeds. They are also more susceptible to having the eye actually become dislocated from its position in the skull. A "popped eye" requires immediate professional attention if it is to be saved. A clean, wet towel should be placed over the eye to keep it moist. Dehydration will certainly lead to surgical removal. The dog should then be rushed immediately to the veterinarian.

Frostbite

When a dog is exposed to freezing temperatures for a long time, there is always the possibility of frostbite. The areas most likely to be frostbitten are those that have little or no hair as well as the ears and tail tip, which have a limited blood supply.

The affected areas should be warmed with moist heat, which will help to restore circulation. Frequently the skin may turn very dark, which means the tissue is dead. If this happens, see a veterinarian for further treatment.

Occasionally, if damage from frostbite is severe, part of the tail or ear tips may fall off. Professional attention should be sought before this happens.

Heatstroke

Heatstroke is caused by the inability of the body to maintain its normal temperature because of the environmental heat. It is often caused by keeping a dog in a locked car parked in the sun, or by keeping it in any hot area without adequate ventilation.

Prompt treatment is urgent. Body temperatures often reach 107°F/41.5°C, and without quick cooling, severe brain damage and death will occur.

Your first goal is to cool the body by immersing the dog in a cold water bath or running a garden hose on the body. Either treatment should be continued for at least 30 minutes. Then apply ice packs to the head and keep them in place while transporting to a veterinarian. Heatstroke can be prevented by making sure your dog has plenty of shade and ventilation. If heatstroke occurs, prompt veterinary attention is important.

Hypothermia

Exposure to either cold water or freezing temperatures can cause hypothermia, or subnormal body temperatures. Survival will depend on how low the body temperature drops. A dog's normal body temperature is 100-101°F/38°C. If it drops below 90°F/32°C for any length of time, normal bodily functions will be severely impaired.

First aid treatment at home requires getting the dog warm again with blankets, hot water bottles, or a heating pad. Hypothermia always requires veterinary attention as soon as initial efforts to warm the dog have been made.

Poisoning

Dogs are curious creatures and like to investigate, which leads to many accidental poisonings each year. Often a dog will find an open can or bottle of some chemical and, accidentally or on purpose, spill it. Naturally the chemical gets on its fur and paws, and while licking the area clean, it swallows the possibly toxic substance. It is your responsibility to keep all potentially toxic products tightly closed and out of reach of your dog.

Poisoning symptoms are many and varied, as the toxic substance can be swallowed, absorbed through the skin, or inhaled. Learn to recognize the signs (listed on pages 180-186.) It's unlikely you will be on the scene when the incident occurs.

Basic emergency treatment for different poisons is as varied as the symptoms, so if at all possible, try to determine the poisoning agent. This is important because what is correct first aid for one is the wrong treatment for another.

For instance, if the poisoning agent is a corrosive or a petroleum product, you want to forestall vomiting since the returning chemical will cause further irritation and more severe burns. By giving olive oil or egg whites, you are attempting to bind, or tie up, the chemical so it will not be absorbed.

However, if the chemical is not a corrosive or petroleum product, vomiting should be induced in order to empty the stomach of the poison. Of course, it is unlikely that you will see the poison being swallowed, so in either case, professional help should be sought immediately. If the dog has vomited, the material should be taken with you to the veterinarian for analysis. The vet will also want you to bring the suspected poison container.

It is appropriate to mention here the existence of the National Animal Poison Control Center located in Urbana, Illinois. The NAPCC was formed to help pet owners with potential poisoning problems. The center can be reached by dialing 1-800-548-2423. This center can tell you the appropriate treatment and proper antidote to give your dog until you can get it to the veterinarian.

Ornamental houseplants can also be dangerous to a dog. It is safe to assume that all common houseplants are toxic to some degree, some more than others. When you consider that dogs often like to chew on something green, you see the problem.

The best solution is to place the plants in areas where your dog cannot reach them and use hanging baskets for the more toxic types. The chart on page 51 lists the types of poisonous plants.

Fires are another possible threat to dogs. Do not risk your own life to save your dog. Leave that task to the firefighters or those trained in rescue.

If your dog does suffer from smoke inhalation, get it away from the smoky area and into the fresh air. If it is conscious, flush the eyes with dilute boric acid solution or plain water.

If the animal is not breathing or if the heart is not beating, use artificial respiration and/or CPR. If the smoke is intense, the airway and lungs may also be seriously damaged by inhalation of smoke and heated air. Burned lungs collect fluid, causing shortness of breath. To ease breathing, the dog's head should be kept higher than its body. Also, a burned airway may swell shut; it is imperative to keep this airway open. Immediate professional help is necessary.

Carbon monoxide poisoning can be caused by faulty heaters, but it is often due to our own carelessness. Dogs often suffer carbon monoxide poisoning from being transported in car trunks. This is dangerous and inhumane. Characteristic signs are depression, lack of coordination, heavy panting, deep red gums, and possibly convulsions. Oxygen is needed immediately and the dog should be taken to a veterinarian at once. If there is no heartbeat or respiration, CPR is essential.

Puncture Wound

A puncture wound may be difficult to see because it is often covered with hair. The first sign may be a limp if it is on the leg or paw, or slightly blood-tinged fur on other parts of the body. The most common location for puncture wounds is the bottom of the paw. These wounds frequently bleed heavily because the blood vessels are so close to the surface.

If it is a body wound, you can see the extent of the injury more clearly after you have clipped the hair around the area. After cleaning the wound with 3% hydrogen peroxide, examine for an imbedded foreign object, such as a splinter or shard of glass, and remove it if possible. Puncture wounds are deceptive; they can be deeper than they look. These deep wounds often damage muscle tissue, causing fluid to accumulate. It is best to leave the wound open so it can drain. This minimizes the risk of infection and swelling.

An exception to leaving the wound open would be excessive bleeding or a chest wound. Chest wounds can be very serious. If there is a hole through the entire chest wall, a "sucking" noise will be heard as the dog breathes. The act of breathing causes outside air to rush into the chest and around the lungs, causing lung collapse.

Your first priority is to seal the hole quickly to keep air from entering. If a foreign object such as a stick or an arrow is in the chest, do not attempt to pull it out. This could open the hole and lead to lung collapse. Just bandage tightly around the object and take the dog to the vet immediately.

Shock

Shock is extremely serious; it is the number one killer in accidents. It is a reaction to heavy internal or external bleeding or any serious injury that "scares" the body (for example, a large wound or amputation with heavy blood loss).

The body tries to compensate for the loss by speeding up the heart rate to keep the blood pressure from falling. At the same time, the blood vessels that supply the outside of the body narrow. This is to conserve blood so vital organs can continue to receive their normal blood supply.

However, if there is heavy blood loss or other serious injury, the body overreacts and causes a pooling of blood in the internal organs. This can cause death due to a drop in external blood pressure and possible oxygen starvation of the brain. Pale gums or cold extremities indicate shock.

When shock is present, you want to reverse the process. Elevate the hindquarters to allow more blood to reach the brain. Stop visible bleeding to prevent a drop in blood pressure. Wrap the dog in a blanket with hot water bottles to help keep the body temperature up. This is necessary because the external blood vessels become constricted and the outside of the body becomes very cold due to lack of normal blood flow. Raising the temperature of the outside of the body helps conserve heat.

Treatment for shock cannot hurt your dog and may save its life. If in shock, your dog should be taken to the veterinarian as soon as possible.

Unconsciousness

If the dog is unconscious, it is important to check its vital signs immediately. Is it breathing? Watch its chest for movement. If the dog is not breathing, artificial respiration must be performed.

Is the heart beating? If not, perform CPR. This is a combination of artificial respiration and cardiac massage. It may take time. It should be continued until the dog is breathing well by itself, or until you can get it to a vet. It should be continued on the way. Your continued efforts may save its life.

If the dog is not breathing and/or the heart is not beating, before starting treatment make sure the airway is clear. Remove any foreign material and extend the neck so the dog will be able to breathe. Your first priority is to get the heart beating and the dog breathing.

Watch for shock. In shock cases, the circulation to the external parts of the body is greatly diminished. Examine the gums and the inside of the upper lip. If they're white or very pale, shock is almost certainly present. Start treatment immediately. Shock is the number one killer in accidents.

Vomiting

Vomiting is one of the most commonly encountered problems in veterinary medicine. It is nature's way of permitting the dog to rid its stomach of an irritating substance, such as spoiled food. But not all vomiting is due to simple irritation. More serious causes are viral infections or diseases of the liver, pancreas, or kidney. Initial home treatment should be conservative.

Food and water should be withheld for at least 12 hours to give the stomach time to rest and heal. Pepto-Bismol® is beneficial because it coats the irritated stomach lining.

After 12 hours, offer water a little at a time. Drinking too much or too fast can lead to more vomiting. The first meal should consist of a small amount of boiled ground beef, chicken, or lamb along with cooked rice and cottage cheese. This is bland and easily digested. If this is held down, a transition to the regular diet can be made over the next two days by mixing increasing quantities of regular dog food with the ground beef mixture.

You should seek professional help if there are signs of bleeding or if the dog is depressed and still vomiting after initial efforts at control have failed.

FIRST AID SUPPLIES FOR YOUR DOG

Adhesive tape, 1-inch and 2-inch rolls

Gauze bandage, 1-inch and 2-inch rolls

Rectal thermometer

Sterile gauze pads

Scissors

Triangular muslin bandage

2-inch and 3-inch strips of clean cloth, 2-4 feet long

Safety pins

Wooden ruler or tongue depressor for use with a tourniquet

Wooden paint-mixing sticks for splints

3% hydrogen peroxide

Kaopectate®

Pepto-Bismol®

Antibacterial ointment for skin (Bacitracin)

Plastic or nylon eye-dropper or dose syringe

Eye wash

Razor blade

Ice bags (or chemical ice pack)

Empty distilled water or gallon milk containers for holding hot water

Blanket

Towels

4-5 feet of ¼- or ⅜-inch nylon rope for restraint

Wire cutters

Pliers

Cotton batting

Tweezers

221

Index

Index